Picked

FOR A
PURPOSE

Picked
FOR A
PURPOSE

Bearing fruit through times of hardship

MEL MENZIES

British Library Cataloguing in Publication Data
A catalogue record for this book is available from the British Library.
ISBN 978-1-912863-04-4

Cover design by Esther Kotecha
Art direction by Sarah Grace
Printed in the UK by Bell and Bain Ltd, Glasgow

What others are saying about
Picked for a Purpose

Mel Menzies has an impressive track record with her books. She has the ability to be searingly transparent about her life experiences, and this serves as a mirror to the reader with the invitation to view their own challenges in a hope-filled way. Look in the mirror of *Picked for a Purpose* and it may prove life changing!

David Coffey OBE
Global Ambassador BMS World Mission

We lived on the same road as Mel and her family. That was more than fifty years ago. Little did we know then what the future held for her – her achievements and anxieties, her burdens and blessings. *Picked for a Purpose* now shares the story of her private and public life. It is Mel's personal faith and trust in the Lord that makes the vital difference. There would be many times when she felt unable to cope with the situation and sadness she was facing. Then she would discover that God was able, through his power at work in her life, to transform the burden into a blessing. This book is not only a personal testimony but also an inspiration for the readers to discover that the Lord is able to bring a similar blessing to them.

Michael Cole
Author and Broadcaster

Life isn't straightforward, an upward trek, always progressing. It throws us curve balls, unexpected challenges, gut wrenching shocks, traumas and tragedies. But God walks with us through it all. Mel writes with honesty and openness, and her words are laced with hope: we are ordinary, but not useless, lonely, but never alone. Read this book and find hope rather than clichés, substance rather than slogans. Highly recommended.

Jeff Lucas
Author, International Speaker and Broadcaster

Picked for a Purpose is a very honest approach to the retelling of a life story, a journey of faith. There is a steadiness in the recounting of fact supported by a wealth of relevant biblical references. The reflections and challenging questions at the end of each chapter, encourage the reader to focus the mind and find answers that are unique to themselves. This leads to a greater understanding of oneself and a faith that is life changing. This book brings one closer to a God of mercy and love in whom we are able to find hope and healing. A sincere, compelling read.

Marjorie Broadhead
Retired Headmistress and OFSTED Reporting Inspector

This is a book which most people will resonate with in some way or other. It can be read primarily as an autobiography, not just a good read but also a window into a time gone by, when times were hard after World War 2 up to the present day, where the pressures are very different but every bit as difficult. It demonstrates how God was present throughout the author's life. However, this book can also be read as a series of short autobiographical stories, which allow reflection on our own lives and how we can learn from the past to shape our futures with God's help. The author deals with some of the hardest things we have to face including physical illness from birth, difficult family relationships, marital breakdown and the loss of a child. These are things that may make some question their faith but the author recognises God at work in her life and her faith goes from strength to strength. The reflections at the end of each chapter encourage the reader to see the hand of God in their own life and to question some of our attitudes and actions.

Tessa Barton
General Practitioner

Acknowledgements

It is with grateful thanks that I acknowledge the encouragement and support I receive in every way from my daughters and son-in-law, while that of my husband is beyond measure. What is also abundantly clear, as you read my memoirs, is that of those who have been at my side as I've faced the vicissitudes of life – so a huge thank you is due to my good friends, Michael and Stephanie Cole, David Coffey and Andrew Green. Also to Marjorie Broadhead, Tessa Barton and Jeff Lucas. And, of course, to my publishers, Malcolm Down and Sarah Grace.

Contents

Dedication

**THIS BOOK IS DEDICATED TO THE WORK OF
THE PRINCE'S TRUST**

Founded by the Prince of Wales in 1976 to help 11- to 30-year-olds
who are unemployed or struggling at school, it has empowered
more than 58,000 young people to transform their lives in the last
year alone.

**All royalties and proceeds from the sale of this book will be
donated to the charity.**

My Purpose in Writing This Book

Have you ever felt useless? A waste of space? As if nothing you do has any meaning or purpose? Ever thought you didn't fit in? In your family? At school? At work? Or that everyone else was more successful? While you . . .? Well!

These are the questions I ask when I'm invited to give my testimony and, be they men or women in my audience, people with a faith or with none, the response never ceases to surprise me. At first, with obvious embarrassment, they'll keep their heads down glancing surreptitiously at one another. Then, in response to the second question, a hand or two will go up. A few more will follow suit for the third question. And a host of others for the fourth. Until, eventually, almost all the audience is participating, laughing awkwardly about their admission yet – I feel sure – relieved to see that they are not alone.

Which is when I tell them that I, too, am one of them. That it's a condition that afflicts us all at times. That we must, every one of us, learn about the truth of our salvation. Our purpose in life. And that it is only in doing so that we'll also learn to counter the negative. It's then, in the hope that others will recognise themselves in what I have to say, that I begin to tell my story.

I suppose it was the letters that were the trigger. First for my depression. Then for my understanding. Small, blue, folded airmails that bore my mother's name on them, they had remained in her keeping for years until she asked me, as her firstborn, to take care of them. Allegedly love letters written by my father during the war, they proved to be nothing of the sort. Or at least, not as far as I was concerned! Rather, they shed light on my beginnings, drawing out of the shadows the hidden depths of my childhood and much that had shaped my adult life for good and ill. And thus began a search into my past in written form: a memoir titled *Me and Daddy, Daddy and Me*, which I began but never completed.

Then one morning – that time of day when I hear God speaking to me most clearly – I woke with a new title in mind. Given that all the books I've ever written have begun life with a three- or five-word heading summarising the theme, it was with a sense of excitement that I had to acknowledge its importance.

Picked for a purpose

As a result, that earlier book has now metamorphosed into this one, newly titled *Picked for a Purpose*. What follows is no longer solely a personal memoir. With reflections added to each chapter, in which I look back and analyse the past, my hope is that it will at least stretch and enrich your mind but, better still, that you will find meaning and purpose in your life – and that of others – as you learn about mine.

The fact is that we live in a world where mental health, bullying, and self-deprecation are escalating. Social media is, rightly, seen to be culpable. To my mind, given that it has the ability to make each one of us believe ourselves to be omnipresent (my tweets may be seen across the world) and omniscient (via Google I can 'prove' my knowledge to be far superior to yours) it is the modern equivalent of the Tower of Babel and may, quite possibly, lead to our ultimate downfall.

Likewise, the breakdown in family life and absent fathers is cited as one reason for the rise in gang violence. Given that one of my daughters became involved in a gang following her father's departure, I find this particularly distressing. God designed human beings to need each other: family and community. It seems to me that in its absence, it's inevitable that young people will look for it in other ways i.e. gangs.

Even for those who are not affected thus, the status quo looks grim. The Prince's Trust states that worries about the future, money, and 'not being good enough' were 'piling up' on young people aged

16 to 25 and that they are the 'unhappiest generation for a decade'. I find that incredibly distressing. My aim, my passion, my purpose in writing *Picked for a Purpose* is to see this book countering the sense of inferiority and powerlessness that is engendered in so many.

My own life has been one of prolonged and painful problems: a dumbed-down childhood (when my intestinal pain went unrecognised), a dunce (school reports: 'could do better'), an adolescent disaster (conceiving out of wedlock), an adulterous husband, divorce, debt, a drug-addicted daughter and her subsequent death. The message I now want to share is that the Lord brought me through each stage to victory, validating the truth behind his promise that *'all things work together for good for those who love God'*.

The fact is, as I realised when emerging from my depression, that we are ALL picked for a purpose. It's simply a matter of learning what that is. We were created by our Creator God, in his image! We are thus beings of creativity – however that may manifest itself! The fruit we each of us bear may have different applications (apples may be eaten raw, cooked, or reduced to juice) but our purpose is the same: to fulfil the potential we've been given and thus glorify God. And that, I hope, may be summed up in my poem below, based on the following parable of the farmer scattering his seed.

'Listen! A farmer went out to sow his seed. As he was scattering the seed, some fell along the path, and the birds came and ate it up. Some fell on rocky places, where it did not have much soil. It sprang up quickly, because the soil was shallow. But when the sun came up, the plants were scorched, and they withered because they had no root. Other seed fell among thorns, which grew up and choked the plants, so that they did not bear grain. Still other seed fell on good soil. It came up, grew and produced a crop, some multiplying thirty, some sixty, some a hundred times.'
(Mark 4:3–8)

PICKED FOR A PURPOSE

A seed, a weed, is sown and grown,
This is your life, you know!
The soil, the toil till they're full blown
Bring happiness and woe.

The root, the shoot, the stem and leaf
The pain the rain of life,
The sun, your joy, gives way to grief
As struggles become rife.

Nipped in the bud you wonder why
Your battles are in vain,
But that's not true, it's not goodbye
Dark days may be a gain.

The buds, the floods, the bugs and weeds
Bring strength to leaf and stem
A flower appears and, on it, beads
Of sweetness, dear, Amen!

And with it come the bees to feed
On what you have to offer
Let not their need, nor even their greed
Hold back what you might proffer.

Then your blossom grows, and with it glows
A heart so full of love
That all around everyone knows
It must be from above.

The joy you bring makes others sing
You're picked for a purpose see!
The fruit you bear is for the King,
To whom all glory be.

© 2016 Mel Menzies

Scattered Seed: Infancy

1945–6

1: The Seeds of Awakening

A farmer went out to sow his seed.
(Luke 8:5)

Mummy says it's nearly Christmas. The cousins, Simon and Chrissie, have come to stay wiv us. They are going Next Door cos they was asked if they'd like to see the Tivity. I love Simon and Chrissie and I want to go too. The Tivity is the Baby Jesus' birthday. Next Door is a convent. That's a place where ladies in long black frocks with veils over their heads live. Mummy says they're called nuns.

Mummy says I can go Next Door if Cousin Simon looks after me. The babies aren't coming. They're still too little. Only big girls like me and Chrissie can go. Only I'm not a big girl. I'm useless! Chrissie stands on tiptoe to see the Tivity but I'm too little. Her bruvver Simon lifts me up so's I can see the Tivity properly. It's a 'normous glass box. Simon says it's a fish tank. But there's no water and no fish inside. Only lots of little dollies and a pretend shed with lots of straw.

It's so beautiful I can't breathe. Simon lifts me higher and props me up on his knee. Chrissie says the dolls are the Baby Jesus in a manger, his mummy, Mary, and his daddy, Dophus. Behind them are some angels. I know they're angels cos they got wings. In the front, there's lots of straw and some cows and sheeps. It's amazing.

Simon puts me down. We're in Next Door's church and

there's crackly music and singing playing on a radiogram: *Away in a manger, no crib for a bed, the little Lord Jesus lay down his sweet head.*

I know about the Baby Jesus cos Mummy says prayers with me every night when I go to bed. Sometimes it's, *Sorry I been a naughty girl today. Please help me to be good for Mummy and Daddy tomorrow.* Sometimes it's, *Please help all the children who haven't got no food.* And sometimes it's, *Now I lay me down to sleep, I pray the Lord my soul to keep. If I should die before I wake, I pray the Lord my soul to take.*

That one frights me, cos I don't want to die before I wake. Daddy says lots of little children he knowed, when he was fighting the Germs in the war, died before they waked cos they didn't have enough food to eat. Daddy says he used to give them money to buy food but nasty grown-ups took it off them. So he and some of his friends who flied airy-planes used to buy the food their selves and get all the little children together to eat it, so's they could keep the greedy big people away. He's kind, my daddy.

Reflections & questions

My father had been in a reserved occupation prior to the Second World War but, having volunteered for service, had relinquished his career in order to learn to fly in the United States Naval Air Station in Pensacola. Stationed, subsequently, in Burma and India, he rarely spoke of the trauma he beheld there, other than the story recounted above. On his return, once peace was assured, he resumed work in the Civil Service by taking up a post in Dover. It was here that the first seeds of awakening were sown in my life.

The kingdom of God is like a man scattering seed on the ground and then going to bed each night and getting up every morning, while the seed sprouts and grows up, though he has no idea how it happens. The earth produces a crop without any help from

anyone: first a blade, then the ear of corn, then the full-grown grain in the ear. And as soon as the crop is ready, he sends his reapers in without delay, for the harvest-time has come.
(Mark 4:26–29 PHILLIPS)

When we scatter seed in the garden, then like the man in the parable above, we cannot always explain why some of it takes and some does not. The same is true of life! We see it in nature and in nurture. For some of us, the seeds of DNA and personality traits fail to grow, while the thwarted dreams of our parents may actually take root in our own lives. Likewise, people of faith sometimes speak of coincidence as being God-incidents. So while a coincidence might be described as random – an accident, chance, luck, fluke, or a twist of fate – a God-incident is thought to be an unexpected occurrence in which God is perceived to have had an influence. Unlike a coincidence, it is seen, with hindsight, to have purpose. And when multiple God-incidents occur, they may be seen to conform to a pattern, to be part of a bigger rationale.

Those who distinguish this pattern and observe the purpose behind it find it astonishing. Which is why it never ceases to amaze me that in a family of non-churchgoers (what my father jokingly referred to as a family of heathens – though I should qualify that by saying 'so far') I appear to have been singled out for a life of discipleship. But why should God pick me? And from such an early age?

What a coincidence that we should have been living in rented premises next door to a convent at Christmas time. And that my cousins should have come to stay and thus accompanied me to see a nativity for the very first time. Or was it? Could this have been a God-incident? A seed of awakening in my life, sown by a loving God who wanted to open my eyes to his existence? If so, it's a seed that took root. Eventually!

In Ephesians 1:4 we read, *He chose us in him before the foundation of the world, that we would be holy and blameless before him* (NASB).

21

Imagine! God chose me. He chose you. And he did so long, long ago. Before the creation of the world. What a privilege. How awe-inspiring is that? The fact is, God didn't single me out. We've ALL been chosen to be adopted into his family. It's just that we've also been given free-will to decide whether to accept the gift. Or not!

- What seeds of awakening do you recall as having been sown in your childhood?
- What God-incidents can you recall in your early life?
- How, if at all, have they impacted upon you now?

GOD'S PURPOSE FOR US?
To thank God for the gift of his son, Jesus, who came to earth to reconcile us to the Father, and for the seeds of faith he's sown in our lives.

2: The Seeds of Curiosity

Truly I tell you, unless you change and become like little children,
you will never enter the kingdom of heaven.
(Matthew 18:2–3)

I'm all by myself at the seaside. Except I'm not really on my own. I can see Mummy at the top of the beach. She's sitting on a rock near the white cliffs of Dover that a lady sings about on the wireless, and she's talking to Auntie Phyl. The babies are in their big black prams, with sunhats on. One baby belongs to my mummy. The other belongs to Auntie Phyl. They can't come on the beach cos the pram wheels would get stuck in the sand, and the babies are too little to walk. I'm four now, so I'm a big girl. But not as bigger as my cousins.

The cousins have come to stay with us. But they are a long way off, looking in rock pools for crabs and sea anemones. They won't let me go with them cos they say I'm too little. That's because last time I cried when Cousin Simon poked one of the 'nemones with a stick and it curled up. So that's why I know I'm too little to go crabbing with the cousins. I'm useless!

I'm bored! I stretch out my arms, put my head back and twizzle round and round on the sand. The sky is spinning, a big blue circle. It's amazing! When I stop it's still going round. The whole world is spinning. I feel dizzy. Laughing, I stagger and nearly fall over.

Then I spy my daddy. My heart beats fast. He's lovely, my daddy. He has a big black curly moustache wot tickles me when he kisses me. Sometimes he cuddles me, throws me up in the air, and catches me, and he pinches my knees to make me laugh. I love my daddy, but I don't know him very well. Mummy says he's been away flying in an airy plane, fighting the Germs. You can't see the Germs, but they get everywhere and make you sick. That's why you got to wash your hands.

Daddy walks down the beach and calls me.

'Merry.'

Mummy tells him off when he calls me Mel cos she says it's a boy's name. I like Merry better cos, when I was Mel, some people called me Smell.

Daddy flops down near a 'normous rock. I wash the sand from my hands and try to hurry up the beach. But the pebbles dig in your toes and you have to stick your arms out like wings to balance. It hurts to hurry.

'Hello, you,' says Daddy when I flop down beside him. 'Had a nice paddle?'

I nod and give him a big smile. I feel very shy cos ever since I went to see the Tivity, there's been something I've been wanting to ask him. Something Mummy couldn't answer.

'Daddy, who made God?'

Daddy twists my long curly hair in his fingers. 'I'll tell you if you tell me where the sky begins and ends,' he says. He must have seen me twizzling round and round.

I look up. It's very big and very blue. And it goes all the way to the back of the sea and all the way over to the cousins and all the way over to the mummies and all the way over the white cliffs.

'Is there a fence around it?' I ask, at last.

Daddy looks like he's thinking.

'Could be,' he says. 'But what's on the other side of the fence?'

That's easy! 'More sky?'

'And then?'

I laugh. I like this game.

'More'n more sky?'

'Same with God,' says Daddy. 'It doesn't matter how far you go, he's just like the sky. No beginning. No end. He's everywhere. And he goes on forever.'

Oh, I do love my daddy.

'What are you two chatting about?' says Mummy coming up

beside us. 'Come on. Time for tea. Auntie Phyl and the babies are waiting.'

Reflections & questions

My encounter with the magnitude and omnipresence of God reminds me of a Bible story.

Jesus entered Jericho and was passing through. A man was there by the name of Zacchaeus; he was a chief tax collector and was wealthy. He wanted to see who Jesus was, but because he was short he could not see over the crowd. So he ran ahead and climbed a sycamore-fig tree to see him, since Jesus was coming that way.
(Luke 19:1–4)

It was curiosity that drove Zacchaeus, a wealthy tax collector, to want to see Jesus as he entered Jericho. It's always struck me that there was a childlike eagerness in the way he ran ahead and climbed that tree. After all, it was hardly the dignified behaviour one might expect of a male professional! But it is in accord with what Jesus had to say in Matthew 18:2–3 that unless we approach faith with the open-minded eagerness of a child, we will never enter the kingdom of heaven.

Had Zacchaeus not followed his instincts, he might never have known faith. But he did! And as a result, Jesus spotted him and invited himself to dine with him. And it was that event that was to lead to Zacchaeus' salvation.

I was barely four when I had my conversation with my father, sitting on a beach in St Margaret's Bay in Dover. One of my earliest memories, it stuck with me because his response never failed to impress me. There were no glib answers. No quick fixes. By answering a question with a question, he made me think it through. Which, as I've since discovered, is often the way God works.

Throughout the New Testament, we see this is just what Jesus did. Again and again, he answered the questions put to him with a question of his own.

'Where could we get enough bread in this remote place to feed such a crowd?' the disciples asked.

'How many loaves do you have?' Jesus responded (Matthew 15:32–34).

Or, when Jesus slept through a storm and was asked:

'Teacher, don't you care if we drown?' His reply was, *'Why are you so afraid? Do you still have no faith?'* (Mark 4:38–40).

A recent *Faith in our Families* report from Care for the Family and Hope asks whether we allow sufficient space for young people to ask questions, and points to those who suppress them because they're led to believe that to do so is almost blasphemous. Yet to my mind this seed of curiosity, of raising questions, is inherent to human nature. It's a seed that God sows in us all. A seed that, once sown, might yet grow. Don't close your mind. Think of the questions that have been raised in your own life, and that of others, whether in infancy or as an adult. Then allow yourself the indulgence of a childish curiosity.

- What questions did you raise in your early childhood?
- Did those seeds of curiosity result in answers that became the roots of your faith?
- Or do you still have unanswered questions? If so, what?
- Might those questions be dormant seeds awaiting growth?

GOD'S PURPOSE FOR US?
To tend and cultivate the seeds of curiosity that God has planted in our lives, and others, which make us eager to learn more of him.

3: The Seeds of Prayer

And surely I am with you always, to the very end of the age.
(Matthew 28:20)

It's winter and there's lots of snow on the ground. Daddy helps me build a snowman and has a snowball fight with me and Mummy. One day, he walks me across the fields to take me to nursery school cos there's too much snow to take me in the car.

There's a big stove at nursery wot roars when they open the doors to put more coke on the fire. It sounds like the monster wot roars in one of the stories Daddy reads to me at bedtime. Daddy roars. Then he tickles me so I won't be frighted.

The stove is very hot. There's a big fireguard around it so's the children can't touch it and get burnt. Today, lots of the children have wet their knickers cos they don't want to go outside in the snow, across the playground to the lav. The teachers have had to put the knickers under the tap to wash them so they won't be smelly, then on the fireguard to dry. Some of the boys have lifted the girls' skirts to have a look at their bottoms and that's made us cry. It's not nice to be looked at all bare. It's rude.

I want my mummy so I sneak out of nursery and run down the road by myself. I don't know what to do or where to go. A bus conductor asks me if I want to get on the bus. Do I? I don't know. I start to cry.

I board the bus and get off in town. It's very noisy and busy in town and there's lots of people and it's frightening. Does God know I'm here? Daddy says he's everywhere, like the sky. Can he see me crying? A lady comes up to me and asks me where my mummy is. Is she a angel, like the ones in the Tivity I wonder?

'I don't know,' I sob.

And then, suddenly, Mummy's there, pushing the baby in the pram. I cry louder and louder. Mummy gives me a big hug. Then she lifts me up, sits me on the end of the baby's pram, and takes us home. I feel safe.

Reflections & questions

My accident at nursery school was not one I wanted to admit to. Nor, looking back, do I understand how I'd been permitted to board that bus alone. Unless it was another God-incident? Yet these mishaps – what I call the weeds in my life – were a prompt for the seeds to grow stronger. My parents never attended church nor, as far as I know, prayed together; yet bedtime prayers were a mandatory element of my upbringing. Never mind where the sky began or ended, I needed to find my mummy. So that's what I'd prayed for in the middle of Dover. Not with hands together and eyes shut, but simply with a plea inside my head to the Little Lord Jesus.

And sure enough, with what I now know to be a miracle but at the time thought quite magical, in the midst of milling crowds Mummy, the baby and the pram appeared before me. Quite how and why I shall never know. But God's promise that whatever you ask for in his name was fulfilled.

The weeds of fear

Feeling lost – physically and emotionally cut off from those you know and love – has been a recurring event in my life. I still recall the sense of terror I felt when I ran away from nursery school. Setting off on my own, I found myself surrounded by milling crowds of strangers. Nothing was familiar.

These were the weeds that threatened to choke me with fear. But far from doing so, they'd caused the seeds of faith that God had sown in my life to grow stronger. Hence my prayers to him. My trust in him. He, endless as the sky above, is everywhere. We may feel lost. But the fact is that we are never alone; never out of his sight. More than that, he is our friend. Our heavenly Father. The Gardener.

Seeds sown on good soil

These concepts of God's nature are printed on my mind forever. He is vast: the beginning and the end; the Alpha and Omega; limitless, like the sky. He is far above and beyond us – but this is not to say that he is untouchable. He is everywhere: all knowing and all seeing. As the psalmist says:

> *If I go up to the heavens, you are there; if I make my bed in the depths, you are there. If I rise on the wings of the dawn, if I settle on the far side of the sea, even there your hand will guide me, your right hand will hold me fast.*
> (Psalm 139:8–10)

This gives me confidence. It means that we are never alone. There is no situation beyond God; no experience we may encounter that he has not previously experienced. The 'Baby Jesus' I observed with my cousins in the nativity scene at the convent next door to where I lived is the Son of God. He set aside his divinity and came to earth precisely so that he might live out a human life as we do.

It may be that you have forgotten the seeds that have been scattered in your life. If so, may I encourage you to cast your mind back? Put the seeds and weeds in your life into God's hands. Ask him to show you how best they might thrive and bear fruit. Allow my story to shine light on the shadows of your memories. Read my story and assimilate the truths it relays. Read it because it may be that my experience, though different in its events, is yours, too, symbolically. Read it so that you might discern and use your gifts. Read it that you might know the joy of fulfilling your potential and making this world a better place. Read it so that you may parent and teach your children in a different light.

> *But the Helper, the Holy Spirit, whom the Father will send in my name, he will teach you all things and bring to your remembrance all things that I said to you.*
> (John 14:26 NKJV)

- What weeds – fearful or negative circumstances – do you recall from your childhood?
- Despite threatening to overcome the seeds that had been sown, did they actually work out for good and strengthen growth in more positive ways?
- Have you ever shot an 'arrow' prayer to God and had it answered immediately?
- Do you know the seeds of God's presence in your life?

GOD'S PURPOSE FOR US?
Through prayer, to learn to trust in God, no matter where we are or what we face, and to know his presence with us at all times.

Reasons For Seasons 1946–7

4: Rain's A Pain

The LORD will open the heavens, the storehouse of his bounty, to send rain on your land in season and to bless all the work of your hands.
(Deuteronomy 28:12)

Soon after my first personal and profound encounter with the power of prayer, we returned to London to my mother's roots. Images of bombed houses flood my mind: partial walls still standing, floorless rooms with windows – curtains flapping in the breeze – to what must at one time have been someone's bedroom; cellars which would once have been hidden, now revealed to all.

We moved into a three-storey terraced house – one of several that belonged to my grandma, my mother's widowed mother known affectionately by all her grandchildren as Maudie. Our new home comprised a 'front room' behind which was a dining room – both solely for the use of mummies, daddies and visitors – and a 'living room' where we children spent our days, plus the kitchen and scullery. Beyond that was a small back yard surrounded by high walls, in which stood an air-raid shelter. Inside was a copper boiler used to launder sheets and towels, plus a huge mangle on which to wring the water out. Each week, shouting out his wares, a man would call with his cart and a big cloppety horse to bring us sacks of coal. Sometimes the horse would do a poo on the road and Daddy would run to shovel it up to deposit on the roses. It smelled horrid! But wow, did those roses grow!

When the coalman had been, Daddy would fill the coal scuttle so that Mummy could build up the fire to make it nice and warm in the living room. Once or twice a week, rather than use the geyser in the unheated upstairs bathroom, she would fill a zinc bath with hot water so that the baby and I could get in and have a splash and a wash in front of the fire.

Because of the housing shortage, occupation of every room was obligatory. Like everyone else, Mummy took in lodgers, some self-catering, others requiring her culinary skills. An Indian family occupied one room on the first floor. The young mother, Dulcie, was as sweet as her name implies. The large bathroom, divided in two and shared by all inhabitants, formed an additional bedroom for Helena, an Austrian girl who helped Mummy in exchange for her keep. And above them, on the top floor, lived Mummy's best friend, Betty, her husband and baby. Opposite them, and next to my room, was a trainee doctor. A skeleton hung from a frame just inside his bedroom door. To a four-year-old, it was terrifying!

Mummy always said prayers with me each night. She would say one line, and I would repeat it. *Now I lay me down to sleep, I pray the Lord my soul to keep. If I should die before I wake, I pray the Lord my soul to take.* I didn't know what my soul was, but I had nightmares about that skeleton.

The pain

I also suffered, considerably, from tummy pain. What I didn't know – and wasn't to know for decades to come – was that I'd been born with a congenital condition. The airmail letters written by my father during the war revealed that, as a newborn, I never stopped crying, particularly when put to the breast. My mother, it appeared, was told by 'those in the know' where I was born in Scotland, that I was a naughty attention-seeking baby and that I should be left in my cot to cry myself to sleep.

Looking back, I can see how it must have impacted on my mother and her view of me. Living far from home with her in-laws because of the earlier air raids on London, and with minimal contact from my father who was then in Burma, it must have been tough on her having to deal with a 'difficult' baby. But the fact is that it also impacted on me. Throughout my childhood, still in acute pain whenever I ate, I was known as a naughty girl.

'Don't be so selfish,' I was told repeatedly as I sat at the table crying. 'Think of the starving children in the world! You stay there and eat every last mouthful.'

With Daddy's stories of the children he'd fed in Burma resonating in my mind, I could imagine their plight only too well. But why couldn't the starving children of the world eat my left-overs, I wondered? Why was it that the things you hated were the very things that grown-ups said were good for you?

It was just as bad at nursery school where the downing of a third of a pint of milk was an obligatory requirement at playtime. Dairy products and greens, above all, seemed to set off my problems. And thus, my 'naughtiness' became paramount. If I complained, I was roundly reminded by my parents that 'children should be seen and not heard'. Meanwhile, being sent to bed with the threat of a smacked bottom and only bread and water became the norm.

The drain

Life became a misery to me. Crying myself through the tummy pain night after night as a four-year-old, terrified of waking Mummy and Daddy and the new baby on the floor below, I knew myself to be a naughty girl. With the skeleton in the lodger's bedroom next door and the memory of Mummy's prayers, I would fall into sleep eventually, only to dream of my death. Floating in the clouds and looking down at my parents standing beside my grave, I had only one thought in my head.

Surely now, I would think, surely now they would miss me? Grieve for me? Love me? Surely now I would not be the naughty girl I was when I'd lived? Surely now, there would be some meaning in Mummy's prayer for me: If I should die before I wake, I pray the Lord my soul to take. Then I would wake up screaming.

Reflections & questions

Think of it as you will, my parents' disciplining of me was the norm in those days. With wartime food rationing still in force, every mouthful was deemed essential for nutritional purposes. The concept that children should be 'seen and not heard' was common to all, and smacked bottoms and being sent to bed with the threat of bread and water were customary punishment. Like all good parents, their aim was to raise me as a decent human being. So I don't condemn them; but neither can I applaud this aspect of their parenting skills. Children need to be given a voice. It's crucial that they are heard for their own health and safety.

When I sought help and support following the discovery of my father's letters in 2012, my minister and good friend, Revd Andrew Green, spoke of 'nomenclature' – a situation or persistent behaviour by which a person becomes 'labelled'. I had begun my life branded a 'difficult and naughty' baby, and it seems that was to be my nomenclature for life.

The problem of being labelled by others is that you take it on board yourself. Every negative event thereafter had me questioning my behaviour.

'Is this my fault?' I would ask myself. 'Am I the cause of this? Am I in the wrong? Am I still a naughty girl?'

If only I'd known then that far from being labelled a naughty girl: *The LORD called me from the womb, from the body of my mother he named my name* (Isaiah 49:1 ESV).

Or that my name, like yours, would be 'precious': *you are precious in my eyes* (Isaiah 43:4 ESV).

Or that despite my terrors and my label, he would be with me always and he had named me:

> *Fear not, for I have redeemed you; I have called you by name, you are mine. When you pass through the waters, I will be with you; and through the rivers, they shall not overwhelm you; when you walk through fire you shall not be burned, and the flame*

shall not consume you. For I am the LORD your God, the Holy One of Israel, your Saviour . . .
(Isaiah 43:1–2 ESV)

Rainy days are a misnomer

Here, in Britain, the weather is always changing and is, therefore, a constant talking point. People in warmer climes sometimes pity us for the amount of rain that falls – as, indeed, we do ourselves. Rainy days are perceived as a negative. But the fact is, without them, there would be no growth.

As William Blake immortalised in his poem, *Jerusalem*, the British Isles are known as being a 'green and pleasant land'. The changing seasons are a vital element in this respect, just as rainy days are a necessity in order for seeds to grow. Similarly, like the deposits made by the milkman's horse, there must, also, be poo. As my father knew, it's an excellent fertiliser. And though rain may be a pain and manure be disgusting and smelly, these are crucial to growth.

And so it is with us. We may feel as if our life, our persona, has been dominated by negatives. We may even believe that any good seed scattered in our lives has been trampled on. But the fact is, as I later learned, in God's hands these aspects of my life – and yours – may be turned to good use.

- Are there rainy day negative events from your childhood that continue to define who you are?
- Is this 'nomenclature' – the label by which you are defined – something you see in yourself?
- Does this make you perceive everything that goes wrong as being your fault?
- Is it your perception that the good seed scattered in your life is now useless because it has been trampled upon?
- Or have you handed this over to God, realised the benefit of rain, and moved on?

GOD'S PURPOSE FOR US?
We are to thank God that no matter how negative life may seem at times, in his hands all will be used for growth, because we are precious to him.

5: But Rain Brings Gain

Let my teaching fall like rain and my words descend like dew,
like showers on new grass, like abundant rain on tender plants.
(Deuteronomy 32:2)

I'm a naughty girl. I know I am cos Mummy and Daddy say I
am. So I'm going to go and live with my grandma, Maudie. She
loves me. Daddy's given me his brown leather taché case for
my toys, but I'm going to put my nightie and slippers in with
my teddy, and run away. The milkman, with his big cloppety
horse, takes me to Maudie's when I run away. He tells Mummy
and then I go with him. He lets me hold the reins when he
takes the bottles of milk and leaves them on the doorstep.
Then he brings back the empty bottles, puts them on the cart,
climbs up beside me and tells Dobbin to go on.
Maudie's house is not far away. There's a long line of them.
They're different from our house cos we have red bricks while
they have pale yellow. Daddy says that's London clay colour.
Maudie's house is a boarding house. That means there's lots of
lodgers. It's very big cos it's two houses joined together with a
passage underground. That's so the lodgers can get from one
side to the other without having to go outside.

On arrival at my grandma's, the milkman would help me down from
the cart and take me to the kitchen door. There I would be greeted
by my grandma's maid, Nita, and her cook, Edie, and there I found
my comfort. Nita, thin as a rake and with hair straight as a die, had a
personality to match, while Edie was as soft and rounded as her curly
permed hair. Both, I later learned, had been in service with Maudie
and my grandfather, long-since deceased, since they were fourteen
years of age, at which time my grandparents had owned a couple

of London hotels. And both, furnished with one of my grandma's properties near Battersea power station on their retirement, were beneficiaries in her will.

Well-fed with freshly baked treats – though with food rationing still in place they were few and far between – I would help Edie in the kitchen or hold the pegs while Nita hung out the washing. Later, seated on Maudie's knee and listening to *Music While You Work* on the wireless, or fulfilling my instruction to stand guard to see that the window cleaner didn't miss a corner, I knew myself to be loved. Sometimes the cousins would visit, and Chrissie and I would watch as Simon repeatedly pressed button B on the telephone in the hall to see if any loose change would be forthcoming. At the end of the day, I retired to bed on the chaise longue at the bottom of Maudie's double bed, and snuggled up with her in the morning on her lovely feather-filled mattress. Thus, cuddled and cosseted, I would return home in a happier frame of mind than I'd left it.

Watering the seeds of imagination

My pain – physical, mental and emotional – was hard to take. But even in the midst of the dark days of my childhood depression, there was light to be found. Rainy days there were aplenty but, like the seeds they watered, far from being a cause of dismay they brought welcome refreshment to my life. At home, where my mother's best friend lived on the top floor, I would help to bath her baby, wrap him in a shawl and lay him in a wooden drawer. This would then be passed through the window of the third floor and placed, carefully, on a little platform, built especially for the purpose, on the two-storey roof below, so that he would benefit from the 'fresh air'. What marvels must he see from there, I wondered? Though given the pollution evident at the time, I now somewhat doubt the benefits.

The great smog of London, when we had to wear masks to school, had not yet occurred, but coal fires still meant that when you blew your nose your hanky would be black with pollutants. My parents bought a little two-door Ford Anglia to replace the Austin 7 they'd previously owned, so trips out of London to the cleaner air of the seaside or countryside were a regular weekend occurrence. Paddling in our little knitted swimsuits in Brighton, Bognor or Eastbourne, the baby and I were in our element. Afterwards, Daddy would help me build huge sandcastles or dam streams, while Mummy looked on from her deckchair cuddling the baby on her lap. Sometimes, we'd go to Virginia Water. Or Box Hill, where Daddy and I would race each other while Mummy struggled uphill with the baby.

Frequent visits to and from my cousins also meant endlessly imaginative games: doctors and nurses, mummies and daddies, catch me if you can, and forty-forty. Sometimes, left to count when I was 'It' and my cousins were hiding, I'd become engrossed in a book and forget to shout 'coming, ready or not'. Needless to say, I'd be in trouble! But time spent at Auntie Phyl's home, where her love and compassion for my plight meant that milk and greens, though on the menu, were never an obligatory part of my meal, was always rewarding.

Holding me by the hand, Cousin Simon would take me train-spotting. Back at home, he'd show me his stamp collection, or his ant farm – an aquarium filled with soil and insects through which amazing patterns and tunnels created by its inhabitants were visible. His sister, Chrissie, meanwhile, an earnest devourer of books, introduced me to the joys of reading. This was to be a seed well-watered, which was to take root, blossom and bear fruit, long before story-telling became one of the major purposes of my life.

Back at home, however, when the baby developed scarlet fever and had to be nursed at home as the hospitals were too full of the war-wounded to accommodate her, my 'naughtiness' was tolerated less and less by Mummy and Daddy. Children, I was repeatedly reminded, were to be seen and not heard. So, banished to my bedroom, I learned resilience. Retrieving the books hidden beneath my mattress, I would read copiously. And therein lay the means of my growth; the seeds of my life as an author.

Reflections & Questions

It may be that the seeds God has sown in your life are beyond recall. Perhaps, like the people in my audience when I ask if they ever feel useless, the negative emotions and events are a cause of embarrassment and discomfort. You'd rather leave them behind.

It's true, there's a school of thought that says you shouldn't look back. Moving forward is seen to be the imperative. I beg to differ. At least if 'moving forward' entails being in denial and shutting the door on the lessons life affords us. Like the smog and pollution evident in the London air during my childhood, however black it may appear, we sometimes need a big blow to remove it. Only then may we breathe easy.

Despite the fact that the Bible has plenty to say about not looking back, digging deeper we find that this is in a negative manner. In stating that *No one who puts a hand to the plough and looks back is fit for service in the kingdom of God* (Luke 9:62) Jesus is suggesting that the ploughman is looking back with regret for what he has left behind. In other words, he is less than wholehearted in his commitment going forward. Likewise, Paul, when he talks about forgetting the past and looking forward to what lies ahead, means that he must let go of the negative religious rituals that governed his past, in order that he might embrace the future and the freedoms offered in Christ.

I'm convinced that, periodically and prayerfully, it is no bad thing to look back – but only when prompted to do so with a view to improving our understanding for the way ahead. Indeed, the Bible urges us to remember.

But the Helper, the Holy Spirit, whom the Father will send in my name, he will teach you all things, and bring to your remembrance all that I have said to you.
(John 14:26 NKJV)

Likewise, we speak negatively about 'rainy days', but the fact is that rain is a necessary element of life. Without it, nothing is nourished. We see only drought and famine. With the rain comes growth, a green mantle, blossom and fruitfulness.

- Are you aware of negative thoughts or emotions from the past that are polluting your present-day life?
- If you are too afraid to clear these out, could they, like a blocked nose, be preventing you from breathing more easily and thence moving on?
- If you have already allowed the Holy Spirit to bring harmful pollutants to the fore, has this brought to your attention skills in your adult life that you perceive as having been sown in childhood – precisely because of the negatives?
- In other words, how have the heavens dripped down upon you, and the clouds poured out righteousness upon you in such a way that you are able to bear fruit for the Lord?

GOD'S PURPOSE FOR US?
To let his teaching fall like rain and thus allow him to wash away all that pollutes our faith, and to bring growth to our tender trust in him.

6: Sunshine and Showers

He is like the light of morning at sunrise on a cloudless morning, like
the brightness after rain that brings grass from the earth.
(2 Samuel 23:4)

One day when the doctor comes to see the baby, Mummy asks
him to look at me. I don't know why, except that she says I have
bad habits, rubbing my fingers together and picking my skin.
The doctor tells me to put out my tongue. He looks in my eyes.
He pats me on the head. He tells Mummy and Daddy I've been
neglected because of the baby's illness, and to spend more time
with me.

Then he gives Mummy some more nasty medicine for me
to make me do a poo. He says I've got to go to hospital in
Great Ormond Street, London so they can take a picture of
the inside of my tummy. Daddy will have to take me because
Mummy's got to look after the baby. We go to Town on the
train and have a fun day out together. From then on I have to
have spoonfuls of the nasty medicine every day and, because
of frequent bad tummy aches, Daddy gives me more medicine
to help the pain (Collis Browne, Phenobarbitone and Fernet
Branca). They taste horrid.

Sun and fun
Daddy tells me we're going to have fun. He's going to be a
magician and I'm going to be his assistant. When my uncle
visits, Daddy and me do this trick. I go out of the room and
Daddy puts a penny under a card without me seeing. When I
come back into the room, I have to say which card the penny's
under. Daddy points and says, 'Is it this one?' and I have to
shake my head.

'Is it this one?'

'No,' I say.

'Is it this one?'

'Yessss!'

Mummy and Uncle think it's magic. They laugh and clap. Only me and Daddy know that the cigarette in his mouth points to the card with the penny under it.

When the baby gets well again, I've nearly forgotten what she looks like. She's got this big round face, with white skin and lots of shiny red and gold curls tight all over her head. Everyone says she looks sweet.

Do I look sweet? I look at my face in the mirror then turn to see my brown wavy hair which is nearly to my waist.

'Why isn't my skin white and my hair curly red and gold?' I ask Mummy.

'Because you've got sallow skin like Daddy, and mousey hair,' says Mummy.

Son light and the blossoming of faith

It was clear to me, even then, that in Mummy's eyes sallow skin and mousey hair were not desirable. But the fun I had with Daddy, and the way Mummy entered into it, made the increasing difficulties with my tummy at least tolerable. And there was more to come.

Soon after my fifth birthday, Mummy gave Daddy a beautiful leather-bound book titled *Great Short Stories of the World*, which, since his death, I still have to this day. A keen reader and an intellectual, Daddy began to add to the repertoire of fairy tales that were my normal bedtime reading. My favourite, by far, was Oscar Wilde's *The Selfish Giant* and it became the subject of much discussion between Daddy and me.

In the story, the giant has been visiting his friend, the Cornish Ogre, but after only seven years he's run out of things to say. So he returns home to his castle where he finds the children of the village playing in his garden among the blossoming trees and flowers.

Gripped with fury he roars, *'My garden is my garden,'* and he makes it clear that no one is to play there but himself.

The children run away, the giant builds a wall and erects a notice saying *Trespassers Will Be Prosecuted.*

From then on, the giant's garden is in perpetual winter. Saddened, he watches the progression of the seasons in the village and surrounding countryside, but no blossom or flowers ever appear in his garden. Indeed, *'only the North Wind blows, the Frost, the Hail and the Snow danced through the trees'.*

Then one day, the giant hears a linnet singing. Looking out of his window, he beholds a sight of wonder and joy. The children have crept in through a hole in the wall and the trees in the garden are full of blossom. Except for one!

Beneath that tree is a small boy in tears because, despite the tree reaching down and attempting to help him, the child is too small to climb up. Down runs the giant and lifts him into the tree, which promptly breaks into blossom. The little boy kisses the giant, who then knocks down the wall and tells the children they are free to play there. *'My garden is your garden,'* he says. From then on normal seasons are resumed; the giant plays with the children but is saddened that he never sees the little boy again.

Until one day in winter, he looks out and the child's tree is in blossom. He runs down but, as he approaches, he sees marks on the boy's hands and feet and his face grows red with anger.

'Who hath dared to wound thee?' cried the giant. 'Tell me that I may slay him with my big sword.'

'Nay!' answered the child, 'but these are the wounds of Love.'

'Who art thou?' said the giant, and a strange awe fell on him, and he knelt before the little child.

And the child smiled on the giant, and said to him, 'You let me play once in your garden, to-day you shall come with me to my garden, which is Paradise.'

And when the children ran in that afternoon, they found the giant lying dead under the tree, all covered with white blossoms.

Reflections & Questions

Oscar Wilde wrote *The Selfish Giant* not as a story for children but as a fable for adults. In bringing that story to my attention, God clearly had much to teach me. As he does all of us. I still use it to this day to demonstrate the craft of writing when speaking to school children or writers' groups, and it continues to move me to tears. Even the ninety primary school children to whom I spoke recently recognise the theme of selfishness equating to winter of the soul, and the generosity of spirit to sunshine and flowers. The love that blossoms in the giant's heart speaks volumes, as does his recognition of something, someone, beyond the norm. Someone awesome. And the small boy's declaration of love – won not by power or might, but by the innocence of a child; by the pain of wounds inflicted upon him . . . Who could fail to respond?

To this day, I marvel! The giant's deeds of generosity in knocking down the wall and opening his garden for the benefit of the children were matters of the heart and soul. No intellectual or physical pressure was brought to bear upon him. Nor did he have any idea that his action was overseen by the Lord of Creation, or that it would lead to reward: the reward of ending his days in Paradise. It was simply the seeds of love being sown within him. The Son light being shone into his heart. The blossoming of faith within. And so, too, it is with us.

Author, Dorothea Brande, highlights this in her book, *Becoming a Writer*:

> *The importance of the written word in our society is great. Fiction supplies the only philosophy many readers know: it establishes their social, ethical and material standards; it confirms them in their prejudices or opens their minds to a wider world.*
>
> *The influence of any widely read book can hardly be overestimated. If it is sensational, shoddy or vulgar, our lives are poorer for the cheap ideals it sets in circulation; if as so rarely happens, it is a thoroughly good book, honestly conceived and honestly executed, we are all indebted to it.*

It strikes me that, as Christians, we underestimate the value of fiction. Stirring the imagination, stories help the reader to see beyond mere words: to envision action; to identify our emotional and mental response to situations. Since it is action to which we are urged in Scripture – *showing* the love of Jesus, rather than simply talking about it – this seems, to me, to be the better way of conveying the good news of salvation. It was story, after all, to which Jesus resorted in the telling of the parables. Let's give credence to his example.

Acceptance makes an incredible fertile soil for the seeds of change.
Steve Maraboli

- Was your childhood one of sun and fun, sunshine and showers? Or did dark days dominate?
- What Son-light – comforts – do you recall from the dark days of your childhood?
- Did story-telling feature in your childhood? If so, do you recall the moral issues that were represented?
- How has story, drama, or film affected your way of thinking for better or worse?

GOD'S PURPOSE FOR US?
We are to be thankful for all that God has given us. And to create a better story by *showing* the abundance of his love and generosity through sharing with others, rather than simply *talking* about it.

Budding Childhood
1947–52

7: Roots And Shoots

As he was scattering the seed, some fell along the path, and the birds came and ate it up.
(Mark 4:4)

Soon, when I'm a big girl, I shall be going to school. Mummy says it's the same school she went to when she was a little girl. One day, she takes me to see it. There's a big sign outside and a high wall around the grounds. Mummy says it's a convent.

'Does it have a Tivity inside?' I ask, recalling the one in Dover.

'I expect so, at Christmas,' says Mummy.

It's an enormous place and I feel quite frightened cos I might get lost. The floors are polished wood, and the lady who shows us around – she's a nun – has rubber-soled shoes that squeak like chalk on a board. They make my ears hurt and my legs and tummy feel all funny inside.

The nun's name is Sister Bennydick. She takes us to see another nun who's called Mother Mary Dominic. It's funny, isn't it, cos the Sister one looks much bigger than the Mother one. You'd think the Mother one would be bigger. The Sisters do the cooking and cleaning, while the Mothers are the teachers. They're all wearing long black dresses down to the floor, with stiff white bits around their face and neck, and a black veil. Daddy says that's so they can only look forwards and focus on what's ahead. That way, they can't become distracted.

Mother Mary Dominic is going to be my teacher. She's very kind and smiley. Mummy says she doesn't want me to do Religious Education cos I'm not a Catholic.

'That's alright,' says Mother, 'Merry can go to the library with the other girls.'

I'm glad I'm not a Catholic cos the library is where they keep books. I love books cos Daddy reads to me every night when I go to bed.

We have to wear school uniform with Panama hats in summer and velour ones in winter. They have a band above the brim with a badge in the front, so we have to have the brim rolled up at the back and sides, and down at the front so it can be seen. Mother says we're not allowed to eat in the street because people will know the badge and we'll be letting the school down.

In winter we wear gym slips and lisle stockings fastened with loops onto rubber buttons on our liberty bodices. You get into trouble if you get them muddy by jumping up and down on the grass verge outside school. I like doing that cos it's fun. In summer time, we wear pretty flowery yellow-and-white frocks with puff sleeves that Mummy makes, short white socks and sandals, and a blazer. When my sandals get too small they make my toes curl under, which hurts. Mummy says we can't afford to buy new ones, so she gets Daddy to cut the leather away so my toes can peek out. But they're still curly and hurty.

The first few times I go to school, Mummy walks me there with the baby in the pram. Then I have to go on my own. When we get to the High Street, she tells me to be very careful when I cross the road and to look right and left and right again in case a tram is coming. That's like a bus but the wheels go on railway lines and there's a funny wand that comes out of the roof and is stuck to a line overhead. Sometimes it sparks, like fireworks. The roads are very busy cos this is London, and one day I get the front of my open-toed sandal caught in the tramline and nearly fall over.

After a while, I meet another girl in my class and we walk to school together. We make up stories and act them out while we're walking. I like that! Evelyn lives in a prefab in the middle of lots of others. They were built because of all the houses that fell down when they were bombed. Evelyn's house is tiny, but she's my best friend and I like going for tea with her.

We have lunch at school in a big dining room with lots of long trestle tables. We all line up to get our food and, when we've finished, the monitor has to collect the dirty dishes at the end of the table until a Sister comes with a trolley to collect them. They scrape the leftovers into the pig-bin – a big smelly bucket. We have rice and semolina and tapioca a lot for pudding, and I hate it. It gives me tummy ache. One day, one of the Sisters catches me scraping mine into the pig-bin and she makes me take it out again and eat it. That makes me cry.

From then on, whenever we have milk puddings, Mother Mary Dominic brings me a jam tart she's made herself. She's so kind, Mother Mary Dominic. I try to be kind, too, but it doesn't always work. One day, when I'm walking home from school on my own cos Evelyn is off sick, I see a lady bent over and holding onto a garden wall. I think she must be feeling sick, too.

'Are you alright?' I ask her, thinking I could help.

But she's very cross with me and I run away crying. When I look back I can see she's trying to fasten her stockings to her 'spender belt and I think she thinks I'm being nosy – like the boys were when we wet our knickers in kindergarten.

After school each day, when we've had high tea at home, I'm allowed out to play. That means I can go on the street with all the other boys and girls. Daddy found this doll's pram someone threw out of one of the bombed buildings and he's put new wheels on it and painted it for me. Sometimes, I put the baby in the doll's pram and take her out to play with me. Her name is Gilly and she's my sister. She's always laughing and everyone loves her. Of course, I don't play with her when Simon and Chrissie come to visit with their baby sister. We're the big ones and they're the babies.

Reflections & Questions

It seems strange to think that, despite being sisters and growing up together, my personality and experience of life and Gilly's appear to have been very different. Yet looking back, I see the hand of God in so much of our lives. Her life-threatening illness with scarlet fever. My having to learn to walk alone to school as a result of that. Her miraculous healing when we prayed for her each night. My need to be independent and take responsibility for my safety – all of which came so early for me. Yet again, I had to put my trust in God.

Likewise, making up stories and plays with Evelyn on the way to school was yet another seed which, sown in my childhood, began to root and shoot. As was the extra reading time granted when I – the only non-Catholic girl in my class – was sent to the library during R.E. lessons. It was as if the Lord was nurturing the author within. Plus, of course, the seed of faith he'd sown in me. I may have been disqualified from didactic Religious Education classes, but I learned so much through my experience and observation of my teacher.

In yet another God-incident when I was an au pair in France a decade later, I met an English girl who had known Mother Mary Dominic and who affirmed my view of her. She was one of the kindest and most down-to-earth teachers I ever had, hitching up her habit when we played hockey, and running – wimple and veil flying – when we had races. If ever there was an advocate for what it meant to be a Christian, she was it. Never mind the ritual of Mass or the Religious Education lessons from which I was exempt! What I learned was not from a book – not even the Bible. My understanding of God's love came from my observing its presence in someone who professed to follow him. Someone who saw my suffering when made to eat certain foods and provided for me.

Which is exactly what God picks us to do! Not to be preachy or subject others to ritualistic religion bound by rules and regulation; but to be seen to be the heart and hands of Jesus. As the Bible says:

By their fruit you will recognise them. Do people pick grapes from thorn bushes, or figs from thistles? (Matthew 7:16)

- Is it your opinion that independence and responsibility should be taught early in life? What was your experience in this respect?
- What friendships and pastimes from your schooldays have featured in later life? Have they taken root, or are they still lying dormant?
- Despite negative influences, have you recognised God's love in others, even though you may have been too young to articulate it? How did this impact upon you?
- Did you ever, as a child, attempt to show this love to others, only to have it spurned as I did with the lady I saw on the way home from school?

GOD'S PURPOSE FOR US?
We are to recognise that denomination is irrelevant when it comes to following Jesus; we are all part of his family and we have much to learn from one another. Even when the kindness we show to others is rejected.

8: Parched Ground

Some fell on rocky ground, and when it came up, the plants withered
because they had no moisture.
(Luke 8:6)

While my teacher, Mother Mary Dominic, was a positive example
of what it meant to follow Jesus, my experiences of faith at school
were very mixed. Despite the absence of input at home (I was now
expected to say prayers alone at night) faith was, without doubt,
beginning to take root in my life. However, while trips to the library
during R.E. lessons were a great opportunity to further my reading,
they singled me out as someone different.

'If you're not a Roman Catholic you'll go to hell,' I was told by
some of my classmates.

Increasingly, as we progressed through school, there seemed
to be a growing element of taunting from my fellow pupils. One
conversation – no doubt overheard from adults – concerned
the merit of a baby's life taking precedence over the mother's in
childbirth. It seemed that Catholic faith demanded that if a choice
had to be made as to which to save, the baby came first. Having
learned, by osmosis from my father, always to look at the other side
by querying matters presented as fact, I asked what, to me, seemed
an obvious question.

'But what about all the other children in the family if they lose
their mummy? They'd be orphans.'

I was roundly admonished by my fellow pupils for my inability
to understand 'Catholic belief' and my arguments certainly did not
endear me to them. Standing and watching at playtime because the
girls wouldn't let me join their game of hopscotch or refused to talk

to me, I felt lost and alone. Only Evelyn was my friend but even she, at times, would prove fallible.

More and more, I adhered to my nomenclature of 'naughty girl', finding a way out under the big high fence around the playground and going to play in the trees by the stream; joining some other naughty girls to stand beneath the twisting wrought iron staircase that led up to the chapel to see if the nuns wore knickers under their habits; or racing up and down the stairs to chapel to see if we could do so without being caught.

Useless at sport, and lacking the competitive spirit present in my mother, I was never picked to be on anyone's team, whether in playground games, school hockey matches, netball or rounders. Neither, it seemed, was I to be applauded academically. Unable to handle the obligatory fountain pen without getting inky fingers, my school work suffered when I was sent to the library in detention.

The facts and analytical capacity required for Maths, English Grammar and Geography eluded me, but I found the creative and human elements of English Literature and History far more to my liking. Likewise art. This was executed in what was known as the Bunny Room. A large ground-floor room with French doors opening onto a small garden area, rabbits painted on all the inside walls, and easels for each pupil, it was inspiring to anyone with a modicum of imagination. One day we were told to paint a 'mealtime'. Most of the children painted a family sitting around a table, but my painting was of a tribal dance around a big pot hung over a fire. For once in my life, it won the praise of my teacher.

Despite the exemption from R.E. lessons, Mass was sometimes obligatory, as was attendance at the First Communion of older children in the junior school. Though deeply moved by the nuns' chant, I felt completely at sea with all the smells and bells. Much to my surprise, however, when I raised the issue of pomp and ceremony versus simplicity with my father, I met with resistance.

'If you had a beautiful picture,' he responded to my question, using this as an analogy for God, 'wouldn't you put it in a beautiful, ornate frame?'

'No!' I responded roundly. 'I'd put it in a simple frame so as to show off its beauty to better advantage.'

Touché! I think the response from someone so young somewhat surprised him. It was, however, a factor that was to influence me thereafter. The roots of my faith had been laid down. The shoots were beginning to show.

Reflections & Questions

Always in trouble at home and school, I wonder, sometimes, if being naughty is either an appeal to popularity, or whether the punishment inflicted upon one might be seen as a form of self-harm, similar to cutting? In other words, *I'm naughty so I deserve to be punished.* Perhaps, in a way, that assuages the sense of guilt? Cutting is also cited as conveying a sense of control that's missing elsewhere in life. Likewise, perhaps my wayward behaviour might be seen as a life-choice: a decision I made, emotionally and practically, rather than one that had been thrust upon me by others?

When it comes to the question I asked my father about styles of worship, it seems that this is relevant to many these days. The church I attend, St Matthias, recognises the diversity of needs to be found in its congregation and endeavours to cater for these requirements. Breakfastzone, Prayzone and Growzone, 9.30 a.m. services, provide the means for families to spend the bulk of their Sundays in other activities, while an 8.30 a.m. communion service is more to the liking of those preferring formality, and the 11.a.m. service is somewhere in between. While maintaining the ethos of church family, this variety is proven to grow church congregations.

I cannot condemn the children who saw me as a non-believer destined for hell. They had clearly been tutored by the adults in their lives. And although the verses below apply to believers and non-believers, they might, equally, pertain to those of different denominations, as we saw in the troubles in Northern Ireland.

*If the world hates you, keep in mind that it hated me first . . .
A servant is not greater than his master. If they persecuted me,
they will persecute you also.* (John 15:18, 20)

Likewise, none of us is the master of the correct way to view whose life should take precedence, a mother's or a child's; nor how we should worship. So much of life is merely a matter of opinion, or perception, politically and culturally.

Blaise Pascal, a French mathematician, physicist, inventor, writer and Christian philosopher, is famous for his statement: *Perception is truth.*

In an analysis of that, Dr Eldon Taylor, *New York Times* bestselling author and Talk Radio host, writes:

*Perception is not truth – and sometimes it is a lie. It is false to
facts. If we are to become awake, it is incumbent upon us to seek
the truth. Truth seekers recognise the many possible paths others
call truth, but they are unwilling to accept the herd definition
and rather continue their journey seeking that ineffable and
perhaps undiscoverable epistemological certainty.*

Nevertheless, Blaise also states:

*If I believe in God and life after death and you do not, and if
there is no God, we both lose when we die. However, if there is a
God, you still lose and I gain everything.*

To summarise, only in Jesus do we know Truth. And even there, we may fail in our perception.

*Who has believed our message? And to whom has the arm of
the Lord been revealed? He grew up before him like a tender
shoot, and like a root out of parched ground. He had no beauty
or majesty to attract us to him, nothing in his appearance that*

we should desire him. He was despised and rejected by mankind, a man of suffering, and familiar with pain. Like one from whom people hide their faces he was despised, and we held him in low esteem.

(Isaiah 53:1–3)

- What is your perception about deliberate naughtiness, on the part of a child, being equivalent to self-harm or denoting a sense of control?
- Is this something you recognise in your life, or that of someone close to you?
- Is there, in your view, a case to be made for glorifying the Majesty of God via pomp and ceremony? Is simplicity a better option? Or are both relevant?
- If you are unwilling to accept the herd definition of truth, are you still able to keep an open mind to the perception of truth held by others?

GOD'S PURPOSE FOR US?
To recognise that our perception may not always be right, but to endeavour to speak the Truth no matter what.

9: A Leaf of Belief

The righteous will flourish like the green leaf.
(Proverbs 11:28)

In addition to my constant tummy pain, laxatives and accidents, I had to contend with frequent visits to the dentist. Not because my teeth were rotten. On the contrary. Like my nails and hair, they were healthy and exceptionally strong. It appeared, though, that I had too small a jaw to accommodate them all and that in order to prevent future problems I was to have some teeth removed.

It was a terrifying ordeal for a little girl! Having already discovered my fear of confined spaces when playing hide and seek with my cousins and Simon dragged me beneath a bed to hide, the dental experience filled me with terror. Held down in the chair while a mask for gas and air was applied to my nose and mouth, I had to endure several visits for my teeth to be extracted. The only solace was the thought of snuggling up in Maudie's feather bed afterwards, while I clutched a hanky to my swollen mouth to stem the blood flow.

However, there was always fun to be had at Maudie's house, where yet another convent featured in my life – right next door to my grandma's property. While Mummy and Daddy played tennis on the nearby courts at Clapham Common, Cousin Simon would lift me up to peer over the wall and report the activity of the nuns and priests. Inevitably, this led to yet another question from me.

'Don't you think it's wrong, Daddy, that nuns shut themselves away when they could be doing something useful in the world?'

True to form, Daddy answered with a further question.

'Ah, but how do you know that the world wouldn't be in even more need if it were not for the prayers of those nuns?' he asked.

If nothing else, it made me think.

As did the Sunday school to which I was sent each week so Mummy and Daddy – and presumably the baby – could have a 'lie-in'. Quite why the baby was never sent to Sunday school is beyond me. A Brethren Gospel Hall, it was to prove yet another seed-sowing God-incident. Many years later, when training to be a Nurture Group Leader following a visit to the UK by Billy Graham, I met the daughter of the Sunday school teacher who had played such a part in nurturing the stem and leaf of my belief.

Things at home, however, were about to change dramatically. There came a time when Maudie, who was diabetic, fell too ill to run the boarding house any longer and she came to live with us. Occupying the ground floor dining room, as had the baby when she was ill, the most I saw of my darling grandma during that period was when I crept up the backyard and peered in through the French windows. A short time later, at the age of sixty-eight, she died of a heart attack and, said Daddy, went to live with the Lord Jesus.

One day soon after, Mummy took the baby and me to visit Edie and Nita who, having retired as Maudie's cook and maid, and as beneficiaries in her will, were now living in one of her properties near Battersea Power Station. I remember, to this day, the vast edifice of the gasworks towering in the distance, and Edie's grief over my grandma's death.

A subsequent tour of the rest of Maudie's properties then took place, presumably for probate. Accompanying my mother, I learned more about my roots. My grandfather, who had died when my mother was a child, was the son of a land-owner with several farms in Suffolk. He and my grandma had bought and run a number of hotels, one of which, Tintern, had been compulsorily purchased and became Clapham South Tube Station (hitherto known to me as 'where Daddy works', though it was, in fact, where Daddy took the underground train to work). Another, The Malwood on Balham Hill, had become the Odeon Cinema, the freehold of which my grandma had continued to own. As a result, my cousins and I had enjoyed free admission to Saturday morning pictures, where we'd sing along to the organ which came up from the depths of the stage, and where the words on the screen were indicated by the image of a bouncing ball.

In addition to the modest terraced and semi-detached houses now inherited by Mummy and her brother and sister, one property stood out as something special. Rosegreen, on Nightingale Lane, was a stunning residence. A listed building with a ceiling painted like the Sistine Chapel, plus murals on the doors (so I was told though when I saw them they'd had to be covered to protect them from sticky fingers) it boasted a staircase to rival that of Downton Abbey, plus a coach house in the grounds.

Mummy, I learned, had lived here with Maudie when she was young. With the onset of World War II, the property had been requisitioned by Wandsworth Borough Council to be used as a nursery for the children of the women required to work for the war effort. Consequently, my grandma, my mother and her siblings had moved into the coach house.

The outcome of my grandma's death was that Nita, who was considerably younger than Edie, came to work for Mummy. This meant that, with a built-in babysitter, Mummy and Daddy were now free to spend every moment they could away from home. And they did! Leaving the baby in Auntie Phyl's care and me with Mummy's best friend, Betty, they took themselves off for holidays abroad. Even at home, life for them could not have been better – and after the horrors of war, who could blame them? Living in London, as we were, cinemas and playhouses abounded, but if it wasn't the flicks they frequented, they'd be off playing tennis on the courts on Clapham Common, or – pre-BBC ventures into *Strictly* – learning ballroom dancing. Returning home after playing outside on the road after school, I'd burst into the house with some news for Mummy, only to find that she was absent.

'Where is she?' I'd ask Nita, full of disappointment.

'Gone to see a man about a dog,' came the perpetual reply.

Meanwhile, other things took over. Music featured greatly in our home life. Before the advent of television, tablets, laptops or smartphones, a family gathering around the piano was an epic form of recreation. With Mummy playing Vera Lynn's 'White Cliffs of Dover', Bing Crosby's 'White Christmas', Cole Porter's 'Begin the Beguine', 'The Lambeth Walk' or 'My Old Man Said Follow the Van', we would sing along with gusto. And when she switched to Beethoven's 'Moonlight Sonata', or 'Für Elise', we'd sit and listen in awe. A keen and accomplished piano player, she wanted me to follow suit and sent me to have lessons. I wish I could say I did her proud but, given that the piano at home was kept in the 'front room' – uninhabited and unheated – practising scales by the hour was hardly an attractive proposition.

It had its upside, however. Hearing my attempts to play the piano, one of the lodgers at home began taking me to real concerts in Tooting Bec, Wandsworth or Streatham Hill, an experience that was to bring me great pleasure and continued for some years. In addition, my mother took me to see *The Red Shoes*, a film about a ballet dancer starring Moira Shearer. Bowled over, I begged to be allowed to join ballet and tap-dancing classes. Sadly, like my piano playing, my efforts came to nothing.

Still less attractive was my ongoing tummy problem. Having joined Brownies with my best friend, Evelyn, we went camping on a farm in Eype in Dorset. Well used to the rigours of outdoor living, following several holidays under canvas when Daddy drove us in our little Ford Anglia down to the French Riviera, stopping at farms en route, I found the Brownie event a somewhat different experience. Sleeping on the groundsheet in our bell-tent with our feet towards the centre pole was fun, as was singing around the campfire where we cooked our food. Best of all was winning my first badge for achieving a five-mile walk along the spectacular cliffs of Dorset.

What was not so appealing was the pit in the ground dug, by Brown Owl and her helpers, as latrines. Despite my experience with French loos, I was horrified. Crouching, legs astride within the canvas walls, was hardly the easiest way to defecate and, in order to avoid the ordeal, I went on a bit of a hunger strike. When the heavens opened and flooded the field to such an extent that we had to take shelter overnight in the barn it seemed, to me, to be an answer to prayer. As was hiring the primary school in Bridport so our clothes could be dried in front of the gas fires. If nothing else, there were proper sit-down lavatories.

Back in our usual Brownie meeting place in London sometime later, I disgraced myself. Unable to face Brown Owl or the rest of my pack, I somehow managed to hoist myself up, climb out of the lavatory window and run home to Mummy. Once again, my dream would haunt me. Floating high in the heavens, I'd look down on the earth and yearn for other than the life I had. Why couldn't I, like Maudie, look down on my grave and go and live with the Lord Jesus?

Whether my mother's piano performances stirred something within me I don't know. But perhaps because of my tummy problems and the way in which I continued to be known as a naughty girl, I found it advantageous to perform by taking on another persona. By creating a comedy character, and acting out a part. Using the metal stand for my father's removable ashtray as a walking stick, I hobbled around and became the *'dir'y ol' woman, from the dir'y ol' gu''er'* (the dirty old woman from the dirty old gutter). It at least had the merit of making everyone laugh. And, I hoped, went some way to reverse the negative perceptions that swirled around me.

Reflections & questions

Looking back, I can't help feeling that the days before television screens, smartphones and tablets, had so much to offer. My attempts at piano-playing and dancing may have come to nothing, but without trying different things we may never know which seeds will take root and grow. Nor what, in due course, may need to be weeded out. Are children still encouraged in this way, I wonder?

And what of the manner in which they deal with the problems life throws at them? There is much talk about the depression suffered by young people today. While my dream of dying and looking down on my grave had its roots in my health issues, social media is seen as the culprit for much of the negative thought patterns that invade young people's minds today. The lack of self-esteem that comes about as a result of having fewer 'Likes' on Facebook or Snapchat? The bullying that goes on?

Could this, as I said earlier, be the modern equivalent of the Tower of Babel whereby via the internet we believe ourselves to be omniscient in that 'wisdom' and knowledge are readily available to us all on Google? And that via the ether we consider ourselves to be omnipresent: my tweets and FB posts will exist forever worldwide. And thus some think of themselves as God-like, while others seek – and fail – to attain such status.

Yet how long before, like the Tower, our self-belief crumbles to dust and our children perceive themselves as nothing? Worthless? A misfit at school? A loner in society? How long, without the faithful prayer of those like the nuns in the convent next to my grandmother's home, before the internet itself implodes and wreaks havoc in the world? How long, with the decline in church attendance in the developed world, before we face the risk of annihilation?

What is vital, whatever our past experience, is that we encourage ourselves and others to realise that endeavour and a moral compass are what lead to success. Like the green leaf, we flourish – and help others to do so – when we're fed and watered in the right way.

By the river on its bank, on one side and on the other, will grow all kinds of trees for food. Their leaves will not wither and their fruit will not fail. They shall bear every month because their water flows from the sanctuary, and their fruit will be for food and their leaves for healing.
(Ezekiel 47:12 AMP)

- Has it ever occurred to you that without the faithful prayer of believers, like the nuns in the convent next to my grandmother's home, the world might be in an even worse state than it is? In what ways have you witnessed or been a part of this?
- Have you ever taken on a different persona – acting a part in order to be accepted? Or recognised this behaviour in someone you know?
- What scattered seeds do you recognise as having been sown and grown as a result of childhood activities like piano lessons or dancing? And what have been trampled underfoot or pecked away by birds?

GOD'S PURPOSE FOR US?
To immerse ourselves in the Living Waters of Life, and thus to flourish. And through faithful prayer, to bring healing to a needy world.

Blooming Adolescence
1952–56

10: Beginning to Blossom

Bloom where you are planted.
(1 Corinthians 7:20)

Despite my fear of sitting tests, when the time came I passed my eleven-plus exam and looked set to go to grammar school, though where that would be I had no idea. Was the senior school at the convent a grammar school? No one thought to tell me that. Just as no one thought to tell me that I'd have to take my eleven-plus again.

In the wake of Maudie's death and the survey of her property for probate, something momentous occurred. Returning home from school to find Mummy and Daddy absent yet again, it seemed that Nita's response, *'she's gone to see a man about a dog'*, was about to come true. Even more amazing, it appeared that they'd bought a house to go with the dog. We were soon to be on the move!

The house my parents purchased was in Surrey, just around the corner from another of my grandmother's properties. A large detached residence with bay windows on either side downstairs, it stood on a double plot. The front garden was bordered with a privet hedge, while the side path, 'for tradesmen', was enclosed with a holly hedge. With the shiniest dark-green leaves and a profusion of scarlet berries, it was a stunning sight. Every year, thereafter, my father strung together small cuttings and, instead of paper chains across the room for Christmas, we had holly chains. A reminder, surely, of Jesus' crown of thorns and the blood shed for our salvation – though it never occurred to me at the time, and who knows whether it did to my father?

With lawns and herbaceous borders enclosed by a high wall, plus an orchard and vegetable plot, gardening was added to my parents' recreational repertoire of dancing, tennis and going to the flicks. And with a prolific yield of apples, plums, damsons, cherries, raspberries and strawberries, my mother was in her element, making jam and bottling fruit for winter, while a huge and dilapidated summer house became a play area for me, my sister and cousins.

For the first time in my life, we had central heating. No more frost sparkling inside the bedroom window; no more billowing, steamy breath when we awoke each morning; no more freezing changes into school uniform beneath the bed covers. As in my earlier childhood, pocket money was not a right but was earned. Where collecting old newspapers from neighbours and selling them for tuppence a bundle to the rag-and-bone man had previously been the norm, I was now required to collect fallen apples or firewood to sell. Despite the continuation of food rationing until July 1954, life was good and an aura of contentment prevailed.

As for my parents, my father was still working in London and my mother, like hers before her, let out rooms. A sociable, sporty, home-loving woman, she loved what life had to offer, cooking, throwing parties, playing sport and games. Highly competitive, she liked nothing better than winning, especially if the game in question, like whist, yielded a small financial reward. Always the adoring partner, Daddy applauded her prowess, praised her culinary skills, laughed when she cheated overtly, defended her if ever she was criticised by others, and raged if she was disobeyed by we girls.

Without a doubt, Daddy was the more vocally and demonstratively affectionate of the two, stroking my hair, pinching Mummy's knee under the table, throwing his arms around us all. He was also, however, very outspoken and highly volatile, flying off the handle from time to time. Frequent rows would occur between the two of them, with Daddy shouting and swearing, while Mummy flounced off to the flicks or to go shopping for the day, leaving Daddy distraught as to her whereabouts, and Gilly and I in the care of Nita who still worked for us. Without fail, I believed I was to blame for these outbursts.

Meanwhile, the buds of faith were beginning to blossom. First up was the matter of my eleven-plus exam which I'd taken when only ten years of age. Having sat and passed it in Wandsworth Local Education Authority, I now learned that this did not qualify me for a Surrey LEA. Bad enough sitting that exam in the midst of fellow pupils in an environment known to me; how much worse it was now to have to retake it alone in a school I'd never been to before. Dropped off by my father on his way to work, I have little recollection of the event other than the large classroom with row upon row of desks, and the fervent prayers I offered to God as I walked home, alone, afterwards. Neither do I recall the words I used, but I remember, to this day, the earnestness and depth of the trust I put in God. I felt at peace.

In due course, my prayers were answered. I passed my eleven-plus for the second time and was set to start Mitcham County Grammar School for Girls that autumn.

The parental expectation of that era never ceases to amaze me! For the past year my sister, Gilly, the 'baby', had been attending St Anselm's, a Roman Catholic primary school in Tooting, sister-school to mine. Aged only ten, I had been given the duty of walking her there each morning before going on to my own school, then collecting her at the end of the day – an overall distance of two-and-a-half miles each way. With our move to Surrey, Gilly was immediately enrolled in a private school. Relieved of one duty, I now faced the fact that the commute to my convent primary school involved a train journey. And despite my youth, prior to starting at the grammar school, I was expected to undertake that journey alone – getting myself to and from the railway station at either end, with a not inconsiderable walk to and from school.

No problem! Except that there were no corridors or toilets on the train. Still being dosed daily with laxatives and painkillers, it was, perhaps, inevitable that I should have yet another accident on the journey back from school. Distressed and mortified, I ran home from the station in tears and was met by my darling daddy. Without a word to anyone, he took me upstairs, gave me the means to clean myself up, and ran a bath for me.

It never occurred to me to question why. Why was I given laxatives? Why did I have constant tummy pains? Why did I have accidents? Why did everyone tell me I had to eat my greens when I knew they made my tummy worse? Why was I constantly admonished for taking insufficient exercise? It was to be another thirty-five years or so before I would have any answers to the unspoken questions.

Meanwhile, the second cause for concern was our dog, an Alsatian. Bruce was about six months old when my father purchased him from his previous owner who, pregnant with her first child, found him too unruly. To us, he was a sheer delight. When he fell ill with distemper, my father nursed him through the night for a week or more and, on his recovery, he showed us his worth.

Put firmly in his place by our black-and-white cat, Beauty, Bruce soon learned to hold back from wolfing down his dinner at night until she had first tasted it. Her kittens became his responsibility. While she groomed and preened herself, he was left to wean them, teaching them to lap, nudging them back to their saucer of milk if they strayed, rescuing them by carrying them back in his mouth if they wandered too far.

Then one day, shortly after our move, Bruce disappeared. The family was distraught! I, alone, was at peace. Sunday school remained a part of my life, though church still didn't feature at all in the lives of my parents or sister. When asked, brusquely, by my parents why I was not grieving the loss of our pet, I responded, 'I've prayed for his safe return, and I know that's what will happen.'

In due course, Bruce reappeared, bedraggled and emaciated, with a rope around his neck. In the opinion of the police, who had received several reports of his sighting by the public, he had been stolen and taken hundreds of miles north. Somehow, it seemed, he'd broken lose, escaped, and made his way home to us. To me, it was obvious. God had taken care of him.

Reflections & questions
It may be that, in an era when men were the breadwinners, my

mother's inheritance and the independence it afforded her became a bone of contention that caused the rows between my parents. Who knows? But looking back, I continue to see that the negative aspects of my life were responsible for the development of others of a positive nature. Discovering the attic – accessed via a wooden staircase from the servants' quarters – I took flight whenever life became too uncomfortable to bear. With boxes and boxes of my father's books deposited there – mere collectors of dust, as far as Mummy was concerned – they would never have seen the light of day had I not made that my retreat.

Escaping from the extrovert activities, the squabbles and the eye of authority, I was in my element. Guy de Maupassant's *The Necklace* and Chekov's *The Bet* (from my father's leather-bound copy of *Great Short Stories of the World*), Shakespeare, Dickens, Tennyson, Wordsworth – I devoured them all, learning by heart great tranches of plays and poetry, now long since forgotten. More importantly, I learned, by osmosis, the craft of story-telling.

It wasn't long before the attic became my writing room. My first attempt at creating stories was for my comic, *School Friend*, then, as my alter ego took over, plays began to emerge. Soon I was writing full-blown dramas. With the help of my cousins, the old blackout curtains were resurrected and, strung across part of the attic, created a stage. Sending invitations to our parents and their friends, we would charge them thrupence each as they climbed the narrow staircase to our new-found theatre in the roof.

Life was good! God had provided the means to deliver me from the distress of feeling a failure. The seeds of my writing career were being sown. And, unlike others, they had fallen on good soil.

If you believe, you will receive whatever you ask for in prayer.
(Matthew 21:22)

Then they cried out to the LORD in their trouble, and he delivered them from their distress.
(Psalm 107:6)

- What memories do you have from childhood about the power of prayer?
- What gifts or pastimes do you now recognise as having begun to bud in childhood? Perhaps as a result of adverse conditions?
- Is this not something we should nourish in all young people?

GOD'S PURPOSE FOR US?
To recognise and nurture the talents the Lord has planted in our lives.

11: Buds Abounding

Make a lampstand of pure gold. Hammer out its base and shaft, and make its flowerlike cups, buds and blossoms of one piece with them.
(Exodus 25:31)

Life in our new home continued to be varied, a mix of fun and frailty, laughter and learning. In April 1953, my father took us to see the Royal Yacht *Britannia* which was anchored on the Thames close to where he worked. It was magical! A couple of months later, on 2nd June, we were all given a teaspoon, which I still have, with a coin in the handle depicting the coronation of our new Queen, Elizabeth II. To celebrate the occasion, we had the day off school, while my parents were among the thousands who camped out overnight in the rain, on The Mall, in order to watch the procession to Westminster Abbey.

I had, of course, been to London before, notably with my mother's school friend who had occupied the top floor of our previous home. The occasional shopping trip to Harrods and visits to Selfridges' Father Christmas, however, were eclipsed by an earlier visit I'd made as a small girl to The Ritz. It was to celebrate the birthday of one of my school friends. Sinking my fork into the cream-filled meringue on my plate, I was mortified to find that, unlike my mother's confection, it was so hard (being made of dried egg white) that it pinged off my plate, sailed through the air, and landed on the hat of a lady at another table.

I'd promptly burst into tears. But far from being reprimanded, I opened my eyes to find that the leader of the band had been sent by the lady to ask me what I would like them to play. Naturally, I'd chosen 'The Teddy Bears' Picnic'. More importantly, I learned that guilt and shame are not always applicable.

With the new house, purchased since my grandma's death, came another acquisition, an off-white Ford Consul to replace the Anglia. Dubbed the 'Fat Car' by my father, a humorous hint of status, it was our pride and joy. Better still, I got to ride in it every weekday when Daddy dropped me off at my new school in Mitcham on his way to work. Knowing how travel-sick I was, he invented games, one being the use of the letters from car registration plates to make up a name for those in the vehicle. Thus a car with LSW on its number plate might be occupied by Lop-sided Speed Walkers. It was fun and it enhanced my love of words.

Life at the grammar school was pretty uneventful as far as I was concerned, apart from the Debating Society. It didn't take my teacher long to discover that I had the ability to make a case for either side of any argument. I'd evidently inherited something worthwhile from my father. Likewise, my ability to act was duly noted and I had the pleasure of being called to the front of the class to take on the role of Bottom (oh, the irony!) in Shakespeare's *A Midsummer Night's Dream* which we were studying at the time, and the privilege of being in the end of term play. Despite the teasing reference to my bodily parts that this afforded (being short in the leg, I always felt too well rounded in other areas) I found my childhood goal was revealed. Thus the usual adult query, 'What do you want to be when you grow up?' was easily answered.

'I want to be an actress,' I'd reply, eagerly.

In all academic respects, however, I appeared to fail both my teachers and my father. An intellectual himself (he later passed the formal MENSA exam at the age of eighty), my grades were persistently a huge disappointment to him.

'Could do better' was the usual comment on my school reports.

But when it came to eliciting the help and support I needed to enable me to do better, it seemed to be sadly lacking. My father's fury with my failure was frightening. My mother became my protector, fending off his rage with what I now recognise as a fellow-feeling in respect of learning. When it came to her aspirations for me, however, it seemed that here, too, I failed.

'Why can't you be more like your cousin, Chrissie?' she would sigh. 'She's so good at tennis.'

Chrissie, whom I adored, also had the fair hair and pale peachy complexion so admired by my mother, while mine remained mousey and sallow. Further flaws in my build and facial features were also highlighted, albeit in such a way that I was encouraged to make attempts to improve upon them – one of them being to pinch my nose to make it slimmer!

'At least you have well-defined eyebrows,' Mummy told me one day. As if that were enough to make me feel of worth!

It wasn't until years later, when I went to stay with a school friend, that I discovered that Mummy's view of me might just be flawed! Standing in the hall, one day, I couldn't help overhearing Lorraine's mother, who was on the phone telling the caller at the other end about my visit. She must, evidently, have been asked for further details, because she went on to say:

'Mel. Yes, you know! One of the Menzies' girls. The pretty one.'

It was as if a spotlight had been turned on me. Me? Pretty? Wasn't it Gilly whom Mummy lauded as the pretty one? There must, surely, be some mistake on the part of Lorraine's mum.

There was fun and affection to be had at home, of course, as well as at my aunt's. It was she who seemed to encourage me more than anyone. Suggesting that I make a cake for my father's birthday, she helped me to do so in such a way that it elicited untold praise from him and from my mother. Later in my adolescence, it was she who bought me my first fashion item in the sales, a lovely swing-style coat. And it was she who, when I protested that Mummy wouldn't approve, told me that Mummy would have to learn to accept that I was growing up and was worthy of such acclaim.

Meanwhile, as a youngster, the freedom I enjoyed with my cousins would be the envy of today's kids. Mounting our bikes, Simon, Chrissie and I would set off for the day, riding around the countryside, hiding in barns, climbing haystacks, or playing cowboys and Indians in the woods. 'Back for tea,' we'd shout as we left and that was it. Despite our immaturity, nobody worried about where we were or what we were up to.

Family holidays on the Continent became the norm and, so soon after the end of the war, we were welcome visitors. Taking the ferry across the Channel, we would motor down in the Fat Car to the South of France or to Spain, stopping off at farmhouses on the way, and – with permission – erecting the old army tent acquired by my father. A big child himself, Daddy made everything fun, while Mummy – the apple of his eye – was full of sunshine and laughter, especially when it came to the card or board games at which she excelled.

Camping under the trees in Juan les Pins or Sitges, Gilly and I had the pleasure of being allowed to swim naked in the Med. Mummy was always there with a dry towel, while Daddy would help us build sandcastles and dam streams. So whether it was learning how to tighten the guy ropes of the tent, making our way up to the farm to fetch French sticks and buckets of milk, conversing with the villagers, or perfecting the art of balancing on the footpads while aiming at the hole in the floor of French loos, the experiences we encountered broadened our perspectives and forged the bonds of our relationships.

For my thirteenth birthday, my mother proposed that I should celebrate by throwing a fancy dress party. She promptly set to with her sewing machine and made me the prettiest shepherdess outfit I could wish for, a beautiful pink taffeta dress with pale-green bustles at each side. With post-war clothes-rationing only six years behind us, I marvel at how she managed to procure the fabric. My father's help was enlisted, also, and by binding a bent piece of metal to a broom handle, he made me a crook fit to rescue any lamb in distress. Was this a portent of what God's purpose for me was to be? Whatever! I couldn't have felt more proud nor more spoiled.

When it came to the birthday cake – bearing in mind that baking was an art in which my mother excelled – I had mixed feelings. It looked good enough, but when I'd blown out the candles and inserted the knife into the confection to make the first cut, I found, to my embarrassment, something hard and unaccountable in the middle.

'Mum!' I hissed, afraid that my party friends would take the mickey.

'Why don't you finish cutting that piece and see what's there,' she said, calmly.

So I did! And even more embarrassingly out came a chunk of greaseproof paper. Was this some error? I felt my cheeks redden as my friends gathered around to see.

'Why don't you open it,' Mum suggested.

So I did. And inside I found the most beautiful, delicate cross-and-chain necklace. My parents' birthday gift to me. Only then did I realise that the cake Mum had made was decorated to look like a parcel.

In the days before digital devices, simplicity was the order of the day. The turquoise pen and propelling pencil set I had received one Christmas, or the gold windcheater I had for another, were gifts beyond compare. As was the simple little gift I received for that birthday. Especially when I later learned that Dad had bought it for me when I was born and Mum had kept it safely for me until now. Another seed sown!

The issue of what, if anything, my father believed continued to puzzle me. Sunday school was still very much a part of my life, but there was no evidence of faith in my family. Bedtime prayers were now left to me, to be executed in the privacy of my own heart and mind. Nevertheless, Dad seemed to hold to ideals that appeared to suggest some deep-rooted personal commitment.

Returning from my grammar school one day, I ran into the garden to find him pruning the fruit trees.

'Look what I've got,' I cried, full of excitement and, opening the palm of my hand, I revealed a large globule of mercury.

'Where did you get that?' he asked, downing his tools.

'A thermometer broke in the science lab at school,' I said, rolling the silver liquid in my hand and delighting in its plasticity.

'So it belongs to the school?' Dad cocked his head to one side, regarding me quizzically.

Guilt immediately cloaked my pleasure, falling upon me like the light-eliminating black cloth donned by professional photographers.

'It went everywhere,' I said defensively.

Dad pursed his lips and raised his brows. Conscious of the fact that this was no defence, I continued, 'We all took some!'

The silence was ominous.

'I could take it back tomorrow,' I offered, reluctantly.

He nodded. 'I think you should. It would be stealing, otherwise.'

Once again, in a manner I can only applaud, I was encouraged to think through the ramifications myself, and was nurtured to reach the correct conclusion.

Reflections & questions

The LORD does not look at the things people look at. People look at the outward appearance, but the LORD looks at the heart.
(1 Samuel 16:7)

Was there a message implied in the precious simplicity of that gift wrapped in greaseproof paper inside my birthday cake? Was God trying to tell me something about the state of my heart? That it's what's on the inside that matters most? That the ugly grease-stained wrapping, like my body image, was immaterial? I don't know.

But like the lampstand of pure gold, there is much that goes into shaping us into the persons we will ultimately be, and sometimes we may feel we have to take a little hammering in the process. My failure to live up to my parents' expectations was evident throughout my childhood and adolescence. Clearly I wasn't sufficiently pretty, sociable or sporty to please my mother. Neither, it seemed, was my academic achievement satisfactory in the eyes of my father. Thus, genetically, I appeared to fall short, in that I was lacking the characteristics they displayed and, despite their nurture of me, I was deficient in the skills at which they excelled.

Were these seeds that had fallen on the path to be trampled on or pecked away by birds? Whatever the explanation, I seemed to find poise only in taking on another persona. Mainly through acting, this was evident, also, when I was called to the front of the class to engage in debate. It was not until decades later, in middle age, that I realised this was probably a form of self-defence. It was as if my unconscious reasoning might be summed up as: *If the real me was not acceptable, perhaps a fictional character might be so?*

Despite my inferiority complex, there was much fun to be had, and much to be learned. We are told again and again in scripture not to make comparison with others, nor to think more highly of ourselves than we should:

> *For by the grace given me I say to every one of you: do not think of yourself more highly than you ought, but rather think of yourself with sober judgement, in accordance with the faith God has distributed to each of you.*
> (Romans 12:3)

We are also reminded that what we do have, of worth, comes from God.

> *Therefore judge nothing before the appointed time; wait until the Lord comes. He will bring to light what is hidden in darkness and will expose the motives of the heart. At that time each will receive their praise from God . . . For who makes you different from anyone else? What do you have that you did not receive? And if you did receive it, why do you boast as though you did not?*
> (1 Corinthians 4: 5, 7)

Perhaps more relevant to my situation is the parable of the workers in the vineyard, which reminds us that we are all equal in God's sight. There is much grumbling from the labourers who signed up first for work, when they learn that those who signed up later are to be paid the same amount for less work.

> *'These who were hired last worked only one hour,' they said, 'and you have made them equal to us who have borne the burden of the work and the heat of the day.'*
> (Matthew 20:12)

Denouncing the comparison as envy, the landowner points out that equality in what each has received is down to his generosity alone, and has nothing to do with what the workers have contributed. Thus, he concludes, *the last will be first, and the first will be last.*

It is, perhaps, one of the hardest lessons for us to learn. While I can honestly say that I never envied others, I certainly suffered a sense of deficiency in myself for years to come.

- The saying, *Beauty is in the eye of the beholder*, first appeared in the third century BC in Greek, while *comparisons are odious* comes from the fifteenth century. Do you find yourself deficient by comparison to others? Or, given that we are God's creation, made in his image, can you accept the bodily appearance you've been given?
- When you form judgements about others, can you accept that it's what's on the inside that matters, and that only God sees the heart?
- Is shame a familiar feeling? Are you able to distinguish between genuine guilt and mere embarrassment, such as mine at The Ritz?
- Do you recall any instance of wrongdoing in your life like mine with the mercury? Were you found out? Did you confess? Or did you conceal the truth?

GOD'S PURPOSE FOR US?
To accept that it's our inner-self that matters, not outward appearance, and that we may need to be hammered into shape in order for our lives to be sculpted according to his will – for only then will we flourish.

12: Petals Appearing

Think of what you were when you were called. Not many of you were
wise by human standards; not many were influential; not many were
of noble birth. But God chose the foolish things of the world to shame
the wise; God chose the weak things of the world to shame the strong.
(1 Corinthians 1:26–27)

It must have been a year later, when I was taken to London to see
The King and I by my mother's friend, Betty, that I first began to
think about creation. Attending an all-girls school, the matter of
the-birds-and-the-bees had simply never occurred to me before.
True, I'd had a crush on one of the girls in the class above me, and
had been the subject of much teasing as a result. But now, with Yul
Brynner and Debra Kerr's rendition of the drama in mind, and with
a dashing young man living opposite our new home, my hormones
began to be aroused.

Discovering that our neighbour's son worked in the City, I began
to find reasons for being near the railway station on his return.
Together we would walk home and chat and, one day, having asked
my parents' permission, he took me to Lyons' Corner House for tea.
Nothing came of it, of course, but decades later, when we happened
to meet accidently in another part of the country, he reminded me
of my schoolgirl crush with much amusement.

Meanwhile, the naivety of my generation, in stark contrast to
today's, was all-too obvious. One afternoon, in the garden room
that housed the gas-fuelled boiler in which the washing was done,
I plucked up courage to ask that most basic yet most profound of
questions.

'Mum, where do babies come from?'

All I learned that day, helping my mother steer the sheets through
the huge mangle she was turning, was that they grew in their

mummies' tummies. Quite how they got there, or how they got out, was beyond me. Far more important was the information that my mother conveyed to me.

'We have a new baby coming next summer.'

What excitement! I could barely contain myself. Another baby! A brother? Or sister? It was only later that a further thought occurred to me. Gilly, now ten years of age, would no longer be 'the baby'!

With a visit to my French pen-friend planned for that summer, and Mum now well into her pregnancy, I bade my parents farewell and set off for Nantes in high anticipation. Jacqueline Godeau was one of five girls and I instantly felt at home. *Monsieur et Madame* made me more than welcome in their grand house where, I learned on entering the front door, one was expected to stand on foot-sized pieces of felt and slide around the polished wooden floors of the hall and reception rooms at all times. Seating me alone at the large dining table on arrival, they gave me a late lunch. And when asked if I would like more, I replied, *'Non merci. Je suis pleine.'* Only later, midst much giggling from my pen-friend's sisters, did I learn that the 'fullness' I had intended to convey translated into 'No thank you. I'm pregnant'.

Daily visits to Grand-mère, who lived with the family in her own room, were interspersed with visits to town, the Botanical Gardens, or fruit-picking in the large, walled garden at the back of the house. An honoured guest, I was always given the largest peach despite my protestations. Those of us in our teens were also permitted, on special occasions, to imbibe a small amount of watered-down wine.

Anne-Marie, the eldest daughter, was an exceptional example to me. Treated with great respect by her siblings and parents, she radiated wisdom and calm maturity. In her late teens at the time, sadly, she was killed many years later as a bystander during the period of civil unrest in Paris in 1968.

Meanwhile, the highlight of my six-week stay with the Godeau family was a vacation in Quimiac, where the family owned a holiday property. Close to the beach, in the Pays-de-la-Loire, it afforded we children a wonderful freedom: shopping, sightseeing and swimming. The experience was, in an odd way, to further my faith.

Shortly before I'd left England, my paternal grandma had given me a ring. A tiny gold circle with two minute hands holding a heart, in which a diamond, a ruby and a sapphire were mounted, it was once my great-grandma's wedding ring. The two hands and single heart were an obvious symbolism of the unity of marriage, but it was to be many years before I learned the significance of the gemstones. Sapphires were believed to be a symbol of loyalty and trust in a relationship, while rubies were considered to be a symbol of love and passion. Diamonds, the hardest of the precious stones, indicated enduring love and perseverance in a relationship.

Thrilled to be the owner of so precious a keepsake, I'd taken the ring with me to France and wore it continually. One day, while swimming in the shallow Brittany waters, the ring fell from my finger. Frantically, I peered through the gentle waves at the sand beneath my feet, aware that gold on sand would be barely visible, and that in paddling up and down I would, quite probably, be pushing this tiny item into further obscurity.

The Godeau family were not, in my experience, people of faith, and I have no recollection of having attended church services with them during my stay that summer. My own budding faith, though, came rocketing to the fore. *Please, Lord*, I begged, *let me find my grandma's ring*. And instantly, I saw a sparkle. Claustrophobic, and therefore terrified of putting my head underwater, I knew there was no alternative. Holding my breath, I plunged down, thanking God for the finding and that the water was so shallow. That answer to prayer was a major event to my young mind, and my grandma's ring remains in my possession to this day, a much treasured item.

Soon afterwards, I was 'treated' to my first taste of mussels and promptly fell ill with what I learned from the doctor who was summoned, was an allergic reaction. A prompt for prayer, once again, came to me naturally and was honoured with an early recovery.

Learning by osmosis seemed to come naturally to me. So while learning French grammar was not a strong point, my spoken French became a matter of great praise from my pen-friend's family. *Tu le parle comme une Française*, I was told on more than one occasion. The problem, as I discovered when my father collected me six weeks later from the ferry in Southampton, was that because I was now thinking entirely in French I could no longer remember English and, for days afterwards, found myself searching for words in my mother-tongue.

Throughout my time in France, letters to and from my parents abounded, from which I learned that the baby who was yet to arrive was assumed to be a boy. Born in August, shortly before my return home, 'he' turned out to be a girl! Holding her in my arms for the first time, I treasured her as if she were my own. Bathing her, dressing her, feeding and burping her, she epitomised all I yearned for as a budding young woman of fourteen. Motherhood! Wearing a grown-up cut-down grey flannel skirt and matching jacket, I proudly took my role as co-godmother of my new baby sister, Kathryn, shortened to Kat.

There was one occasion, however – and a significant one at that – when I nearly lost the new baby. Following a visit to the sweetshop, now that rationing had ceased, I was clearly too entranced with my purchase of liquorice whirls and jelly babies to recall my responsibilities.

'Where's the baby?' asked my mother when I arrived home.

Shock, horror! I'd left her pram neatly parked outside on the pavement and had to run all the way back to find her. Fortunately for all concerned, she was still there – though many years later I was to joke that it might have been better had she not been!

Needless to say, I was, justifiably on this occasion, in trouble yet again. Regaled with my mother's endless entreaty, 'For goodness' sake! Stop day-dreaming,' I knew myself quite unable to obey. Day-dreaming was in my DNA. An endless awe and fascination with life, with nature, with God's creation, drove me to speculate, to imagine, to wonder, all the what-ifs and if-nots presented to my teenage mind.

Soon afterwards, we made a trip to Scotland to visit my Scottish grandparents. Mum flew to Inverness with the baby, while Dad, Gilly and I drove up. What fun we had with far-flung cousins: picking raspberries in my grandparents' large, walled garden; recalling earlier childhood visits when we'd secretly clambered aboard the tiny lift designed to transport food and utensils from the basement kitchen to the ground-floor dining room; visiting beaches on the east coast near Lossiemouth; collecting mapimoos (cowrie shells); travelling on the bus to Aberdeen.

On our return home, we were, once more, on the move again. After barely four years in Surrey, I learned that my father had put in for a post in South Devon. That Christmas, shortly before my fifteenth birthday, we went to stay in a cottage in a delightful, sleepy seaside town in the West Country, with golden sandy beaches on either side of the estuary. This was to be our new home. Leaving Dad to take up his job as Customs Officer and Receiver of Wreck, we girls, Mum, the new baby, Gilly and I, returned to sell our old house. A new life beckoned. As with the lampstand of buds and petals, so the light of God's Word and Spirit shone upon my budding faith.

Craft the centre stem of the lampstand with four lamp cups shaped like almond blossoms, complete with buds and petals. (Exodus 25:34 NLT)

Reflections & questions

Looking back, I perceive the emphasis in my mother's life to have centred on extrovert pursuits, an attribute that – like the seeds that were trampled on – passed me by. As the baby of a large family – she had five brothers and sisters – she revelled in anything that put her in the spotlight, a trait confirmed by my aunt, her older sister.

My father's attention was entirely upon her and it was clear to all that he adored her. Nevertheless, there were rows. His love of art, painting in oils and watercolours in particular, was deemed by my mother to be 'too messy'. Consequently, despite having won a scholarship to Glasgow University in his youth (which he'd never taken up), his interests were relinquished in favour of hers. Clearly, this caused tensions.

More like my father in temperament, I was, nonetheless, the eldest child while he was the second of three boys. It was to be many years before I studied the phenomenon of how a person's place among his/her siblings might affect the manner in which they parent their own offspring. The blog posts I wrote online, titled *Eldest Child Syndrome – Are You What Your Parents Have Made You* and *People Pleasers – How to Deal with Other People's Problems* still, to this day, attract a huge readership worldwide.

Meanwhile, what continued to intrigue me was quite where my faith came from. With neither parent disclosing overt evidence of a personal relationship with God, it seemed that he, nevertheless, proved himself in my life. It was almost as if this, in itself, became a game or a sport, whereby each occurrence requiring prayer was a test of my faith. Thus the accomplishment of passing my eleven-plus exams twice, the return of our dog, the finding of my grandma's ring, and my healing after eating mussels, were proof of his faithfulness to me. Symbolic of his rewarding perseverance when tested, his enduring power was revealed when returning something that had been snatched away; his shining light on something small but precious in the vastness of the sea.

Practice makes perfect, I was repeatedly told when I sat at the piano, and it seemed as if the Lord was affording me the opportunity to practise with my faith. Like my mother's sport, each test achieved results, deepening my trust and broadening my faith.

- Like the candlestick of buds and petals in Exodus, what do you recall of the light shed on your early life?
- What memories have you of something lost and found, like my grandma's ring? Are they symbolic of the loss sin creates in our lives, and the joy of being found by God?
- How do you perceive the idea that a parent's placement among his or her siblings might affect the way in which they parent each of their own children?

GOD'S PURPOSE FOR US?
To thank our Father that though once we were lost, we have now been found and are one with him. Joined together as one heart, we are to develop a sapphire-like trust and diamond-like commitment in him, and thus to know his ruby-like love for us.

Stunted Growth
1957–64

13: Nipped in the Bud

Some [seed] fell on rocky places, where it did not have much soil. It sprang up quickly, because the soil was shallow. But when the sun came up, the plants were scorched, and they withered because they had no root.

(Mark 4:5–6)

For about a year after our move to Devon, we lived in a rented house at the top of a hill. With farmland just over the road and views of Dartmoor beyond, it was idyllic. If I wasn't 'helping' with the harvest with my new-found friends, or learning to ride a horse, I'd be on the beach or 'helping' Dad when he went out to apprehend any smugglers who might have taken refuge in the calm waters of the estuary. Our Alsatian, Bruce, would accompany the two of us, standing on the prow of the Customs' boat and barking at the swans. When he fell in, which he often did, he'd refuse to obey Dad's command to swim ashore, and would paddle alongside us until, with much heaving and panting on Dad's part, he was hauled back into the boat. He would then soak us as he shook off the salty water from his furry coat.

On other occasions, no doubt following the nurturing instincts instilled in him by our cat, Bruce would rescue birds from the estuary. He seemed to have an eye for creatures in distress, particularly those that were unable to fly due to the coagulation of engine oil on their feathers. Swimming back to Customs Quay with the bird held gently in his jaw, he would deposit it at my father's feet. When the bird had been cleaned and fed, it was let loose once more. If, however, it had broken a wing, my father would attach a lollipop stick as a splint, and the creature would be taken home and cared for until it was able to fly once more. In this case, it would adopt Bruce as its nurse, snuggling into his armpit for warmth, confident that should the doorbell ring, the dog would rise slowly and carefully so as to cause it no harm. Once clear, Bruce would then return to natural doggy instincts and rush, barking, towards the possible intruder on the doorstep.

Sometimes, we would be given live crab or lobsters as a gift from some of the fishermen and, on more than one occasion, I had to transport them home, about a mile uphill, one in each hand. Weighing at least a couple of pounds each (nearly a kilo), this required some careful handling, ensuring that not only were my fingers out of reach of those vicious, writhing claws, but also my legs.

Meanwhile, back at home, I had discovered a box of Dad's books I'd never come across before. Among them was one which was clearly a Scripture prize, awarded to him by West End School in Elgin, in 1923. Given that Dad showed no sign of having ever darkened the door of a church, this was a big surprise! Fascinated, I began to read it as soon as possible.

Titled *The Yellow Pup* and written by E. Everett-Green, it was the story of a young boy named Teddy, who had lost his father shortly before his twelfth birthday.

'*You must grow up a good man, my boy, and take care of your mother and the little ones,*' Teddy had been told. So when he came across a stray puppy, which he named Scamp, he found himself faced with a conflict.

Suddenly it occurred to Teddy that finding the puppy did not exactly make it his property. Most likely it had just wandered away from some cottage home, and he would have to give it up to its owner. At this thought Teddy's face grew very grave, and he heaved a big sigh; for already he loved that puppy very much.

Much later, during a conversation about the gentry and their obligation to worship God and *walk uprightly in the world*, Teddy suggests that neither should people like himself be ashamed of being poor, nor of having to work hard to earn a meagre living.

'*Indeed not, my man,*' comes the reply. '*Wealth may be very pleasant, but money makes nobody happy . . . And as for being ashamed of being poor – why that is the silliest notion in the world; and a very wrong one too. For who was it that laid aside all the glory and majesty and wealth not only of earth, but of his Father's home in heaven; and became poor and worked with his hands at a humble trade?'*

'That was Jesus,' said Freddie.

The importance of a good work is presented by the school mistress, Miss Masterman, as Teddy and his brothers seek to find the money to purchase a licence for Scamp.

'Children,' she said . . . 'I want every boy in the land to earn . . . Pride in work, love of work – those are qualities which are the salt of a nation's life . . .'

A court case over ownership of the puppy ensues, but all ends happily and when the boys speak of becoming pioneers in the new world of Canada and Australia they are told:

'First try to become good, honest, God-fearing men, ashamed of nothing but sin, then put your whole heart into whatever task you find nearest to your hand . . .'

Reading that book by torchlight beneath the blankets in bed and feeling as if my heart had been flooded with light, I realised that although I knew God personally as someone who cared for me, I had never made a decision to follow Jesus; to accept his gift of forgiveness and salvation, to adhere to his values and to follow him; to put my trust in him. Nor to put my whole heart into whatever task he had for me. Privately, prayerfully and tearfully, I made my commitment.

Sunday school now seemed to be off the agenda. Instead, my parents enrolled me with Island Cruising Club with the intention that I would learn to sail. A visit to *Egremont* was a must. Once a ferry boat, it was said to have inspired the Gerry and the Pacemakers' song 'Ferry across the Mersey'. But with a terror of being under water (my claustrophobia again) I baulked at the prospect of a small dinghy and the risk of the boom going about and knocking me in. Worse still, capsizing the boat in order to learn how to right it again was quite beyond me. Luffing sails, tiller and rudder, going about, port and starboard – the nautical terms I learned and retained, but it was the handsome cadet who trained me who caught my eye. And I his. With my father's permission now that I was fifteen, he took me out for a drive in his sports car – my first proper date!

As if changing schools when I was in the middle of taking my eleven-plus wasn't bad enough, I now faced further difficulties. With O-levels looming in the not too distant future, I was beset with the problem of being in a mixed school for the first time in my life. What's more, in the quiet backwater where we now lived and where few of the inhabitants had ever been to Exeter, let alone London where I had lived, it appeared that I was an exotic bloom.

My knowledge of sexual activity might be limited to where babies grew, but my hormones and the endless flirtation of the boys ensured that my education was completed. Not in practice, I hasten to add, but certainly mentally and emotionally. Never before had I been so much in demand. Nor so much admired. Nor so much centre-stage. Regardless of the fact that I was an introvert by nature, I revelled in it. And, sadly, it was my undoing.

Who could attend to school work when the boys were constantly flicking suggestive messages at you across the classroom? Why would you want to play sport when there were boys queuing up to make lewd suggestions behind the bike sheds? I learned more, in theory, about the-birds-and-the-bees in those four terms at the grammar school than I did about anything else. Yet still, somehow, I managed to attain six O-levels.

The previous year, my parents had bought the vegetable garden belonging to an hotel. A large sloping plot at the bottom of the valley, and with a sandy beach just over the garden wall, it was everything they had dreamed of. Commissioning an architect, they had plans drawn up and our new home was erected.

With a large dining room built especially to accommodate the newly acquired table-tennis table, Mum and Dad threw parties non-stop. The bridge club and golf club replaced the flicks and the dance-floor and, with a large conservatory in which to set up an easel, my father was now permitted to take up his hobby, join the local Art Club and exhibit his work. In between times, he rotovated the garden, created lawns and terraces, herbaceous gardens and rose beds, vegetable plots and ponds, and both parents revelled in their new-found way of life.

Still totally lacking in confidence, despite the interest shown in me, I was introduced to the wonders of alcohol. Sneaking me into a pub while still under-age, the older boys would ply me with booze. And what a confidence-builder it was! All inhibitions absolved (or perhaps dissolved) I found myself able to laugh and flirt as freely as anyone. Not that I was left entirely to my own devices. Although permitted to attend weekend dances held locally I was, nevertheless, expected to leave at ten o'clock when my father picked me up in the car. And during the week in term-time, no outings were allowed and bedtime remained a strict eight-thirty.

When, at last, my O-levels were behind me, I made a pact with my parents. Whether this was a lack of interest in continuing my academic education, or a deep-seated desire to escape the decadent lifestyle I now seemed to be leading, I can't say. Whatever, my plea was that I might go abroad as an au pair. Having already spent six weeks living in Nantes with my pen-friend's family prior to Kat's arrival, my proposal was accepted. My parents made arrangements for me to live at my pen-friend's home and to work with a family the Godeaus had selected. It was an unforgettable experience!

My employers were well-to-do. As was the norm in those days, Monsieur was the bread-winner. He worked in local government while Madame, ostensibly, was a stay-at-home mother. Except that she wasn't. They lived in a large apartment in the middle of Nantes and once Monsieur left for the Bureau, other men would visit. While I fed the three children, all aged under five, Madame entertained her gentlemen callers in her room. Naively, I took it that they must be members of her family – and perhaps they were.

I, meanwhile, was treated as a servant. There was no attempt to include me in family life. When Monsieur returned, I was expected to wait on table and to partake of my own meal in the kitchen. The full care of the children, cooking, feeding, bathing and clothing them, plus hand-washing the nappies, all fell to me. In the afternoon, the highlight of my day, I would leave Madame to her own devices, and take the children to the Botanical Gardens where I, at least, had the company of other au pairs.

There I learned that the terms of my employment were totally inadequate. My pay covered the bus fare to and from work but little else. Unknown to me at the time, no remuneration was made to my pen-friend's family for my keep, as had been agreed. With essential feminine hygiene purchases to be made, I could barely make ends meet.

It wasn't in my nature to complain. Besides which, in addition to my 'seen but not heard' upbringing, I was aware that any complaint might rebound on my pen-friend's family, since it was they who had made the arrangements for my workplace. Hence, my letters home – kept for decades by my parents but, sadly, destroyed later by my youngest sister, Kat – although frequent, initially made no mention of my plight with my employers.

Faced one day with being unable to pay the bus fare and having to walk several miles to work, where I got lost and ended up in tears, I realised I had no option but to come clean with my parents. The result was that my pay increased slightly and, in return for giving English lessons to some French children, I was allowed an hour or two off a week to take French shorthand lessons.

My pen-friend's family, meanwhile, treated me as a daughter, a special one at that. Once again, the biggest peach from the trees in the garden was reserved for me, as was the largest portion of raspberries. Their house, some distance from my employers, although large and grand, was made to feel like home. There was still Grand-mère to be visited, *crêpes* to be made, the piano to be played. At Christmas, after attending Midnight Mass – my first experience of church attendance with the family – we gathered around the fire and hung our Christmas stockings from the mantelpiece in readiness for Christmas Day, when roast leg of lamb was the French equivalent of turkey.

Nevertheless, after six months with my employers I could take no more and handed in my notice. Madame was furious! The agreement, I was told, was for a full year. I stood my ground and promptly had my last month's pay docked. Yet again, I couldn't bring myself to tell anyone. I set off by train from Nantes and discovered that I'd been sent to the wrong terminus in Paris. Grabbing a taxi, I asked to be taken to the Gard du Nord but, held up in traffic and watching the meter go round, I realised I wouldn't be able to meet the fare. I was promptly deposited on the pavement together with my father's wartime tin trunk.

Knowing I had no hope of hauling it into the station, I sat down and cried. How could God allow this to happen? Within moments a military man in full army regalia appeared. After ascertaining my needs, he called for a porter and, with his wife, led me onto the platform and saw me onto the train.

My new-found faith and commitment had barely surfaced during my time in France, but with this mini-miracle and a second one to follow when an old school friend, Michael, met me from the ferry in Southampton and bought me a train ticket home, I had to acknowledge that God was at work in my life. My Father and Protector, he'd provided for me and kept me safe. I wish I could say that this was the turning point in my coming to know him properly. Sadly, it was not.

Reflections & questions

Sow your seed in the morning, and at evening let your hands not be idle, for you do not know which will succeed, whether this or that, or whether both will do equally well. (Ecclesiastes 11:6)

Like the example of God's love shown me by my teacher, Mother Mary Dominic, I was to learn much from the example of my father. And even from our dog! The tenderness and compassion both showed towards creatures in need spoke volumes. And what a lesson there was to learn in observing Bruce setting aside all doggy instincts in order to protect the birds in his care. Isn't this what we are commanded to do?

But that was not all. Once again, the discernment of Dorothea Brande's statement was to be seen in my life: *Fiction supplies the only philosophy many readers know: it establishes their social, ethical and material standards; it confirms them in their prejudices or opens their minds to a wider world.*

Via the ethics portrayed in the story of *The Yellow Pup*, I was enabled to see a way of life in which morality and service for others were held in high esteem. Crucially, I was led to see these as the values upheld by Jesus, himself, and my commitment to follow him was, thus, a good and honest response. Sadly though, like the seed that fell on rocky ground, my vow was short lived. It sprang up quickly but, having no root and therefore little in the way of nourishment, it was soon scorched and became withered.

Passion and zeal are no bad thing when it comes to following our Saviour but unless they are fed on a daily moment-by-moment basis they may well burn out. Such is the testimony of many who eventually come forward for adult believer's baptism. Without regular prayer, Bible study, and meeting for fellowship, the roots of a relationship with the Lord may fail, and with them the stem and leaf of belief they neglect to feed.

- At what point did you first make a commitment to follow Jesus?
- What inspired you to do so? Was it by instruction? By the example of others? Or by reading a work of fiction?
- Did you then go on to experience temptations such as mine in school? Or trials and tribulations such as my experiences in France?
- How, if at all, did you deal with these?

GOD'S PURPOSE FOR US?
We are to be 'alert and of sober mind if we are to resist the wiles of the devil who prowls around like a roaring lion looking for someone to devour' (see 1 Peter 5:8).

14: Soil and Toil

He who tills his land will have plenty of food, but he who follows empty pursuits will have poverty in plenty.
(Proverbs 28:19 NASB)

Despite the ups and downs of childhood and teenage traumas, my relationship with my parents was one of warmth and affection, and home life, on my return from France, was definitely to be desired. However, Gilly was at a local private school and Kat, now a toddler, was clearly the centre of parental attention. When, that is, parental attention was not focused on bridge, golf, gardening and parties!

My father's disappointment in my academic achievement was patently obvious, while my mother could see no point in further education for girls. Having met me in Exeter when I arrived home from France penniless and starving, she immediately took me to a high-street shop where she'd seen a pink tulle frock – a ballerina-style ball gown – in the sales. Clearly this was of far greater importance to her than anything else, and though I loved the dress, I can't help feeling now that she had her priorities round the wrong way.

'Men don't make passes at girls who wear glasses,' she would tell me, earnestly, whenever we were out of earshot from my father. In other words, being studious was a barrier to romance.

Her purpose for me was thus clearly implied: marriage the ultimate goal. Prior to that, nursing, teaching and secretarial work were the only options for a middle-class girl without a university education, and the technical college seemed the obvious answer. Arrangements were made for me to travel in daily with a Royal Naval friend of my parents.

It was a good hour's journey on narrow country lanes in those days but Clive's Land Rover, the ripped canvas top flapping in the wind, was far from claustrophobic and I never suffered once from car-sickness. That isn't to say that the ride was perfect, however. Far from it! Driving at speed through a small village with no pavements, at the bottom of a steep hill, I recall one incident when the Land Rover literally whipped the broom from a woman's hands as she swept the front step of her house clean. On other occasions, we would veer all over the road as Clive attempted to light a cigarette, sheltering the flame in both hands to protect it from the draughts.

Having witnessed my father's addiction to tobacco, when he would hit the roof if he ran out of cigarettes after shop closing time, I'd sworn that I would never succumb. A hollow promise if ever there were one! In order to preserve life – my own and that of the pedestrians we passed on our journey – I began lighting Clive's cigarettes and, within a short time, became addicted.

And not simply to the tobacco! As I've progressed through life, I've realised more and more how easy it is to condemn without understanding. Cigarettes, like the quantity of alcohol I now consumed, became yet another escape. Armed with a fancy cigarette case and a lighter, I no longer felt so self-conscious when sitting alone or in the midst of a crowd. The act of lighting up, of puffing, blowing and tapping off the ash became a mini-drama in which one could equate to the part of a film star. Once again, my alter ego came to my rescue.

After a year at college, I was ready for work. Once more, my heavenly Father intervened in that a famous author happened to be living nearby and he required a secretary. I applied and was accepted.

A multi-published novelist and short-story writer, Paul Gallico was the author of *Thomasina*, *The Snow Goose* (an allegory of D-Day which won an award) and, most recently at that time, *Mrs 'Arris Goes to Paris* which became a bestseller. Many of his works were adapted for cinema and television motion pictures (one of which became an Oscar winner) and film negotiations for *Mrs 'Arris* having begun during the time I worked for him, I had to liaise with the film makers. It was, however, to be many years before a deal was completed, and Angela Lansbury starred as Mrs 'Arris.

In addition to manning the telephone, dealing with the post, and categorising Mr Gallico's library, my day was taken up with dictation and shorthand during the morning and, armed with a bottle of Tipp-Ex (to erase errors), typing up my notes on a large Imperial typewriter in the afternoon and evening. Dictation, if the weather was fine, took place while we roamed around his steeply sloping garden among the scented mimosa trees – a delight in some ways, but no easy task in that I was scurrying along stony winding paths behind him with a pencil and notebook in my hands.

It was, however, a moving experience! Mr Gallico had been commissioned by a national newspaper to serialise the true story of the sinking of the *MV Princess Victoria*, a ferry that plied between Larne in Northern Ireland and Stranraer on the west coast of Scotland. Setting sail, despite gale warnings, the voyage resulted in the death of every woman and child aboard. One, notably, a nun was en route to visit her family. It was this story, I suspect, that inspired the subsequent writing of the TV drama, *The Poseidon Adventure*.

Sometimes, the routine changed and Mr Gallico would have visitors, notably Baron Von Felz-Fein and his wife. Along with their delightful little daughter, Ludmila, for whom Paul Gallico wrote the book, *Ludmila: A Story of Liechtenstein*, I would be invited to join them. In stark contrast to my experience in France, I was treated as one of the family. The Baroness was particularly kind to me, and would pass on items of clothing and accessories she'd tired of, my favourites being a gorgeous cashmere jumper and a black leather and suede handbag, both of which I treasured for years.

Sadly, it was all to end. Mr Gallico contracted phlebitis and was confined to bed – a four poster, at the foot of which I continued to take dictation. In due course, he decided to return to the property he owned in Antibes in the South of France. Although I was invited to join him, my father's reluctance was evident and I declined.

Nevertheless, as a typical adolescent, I yearned to escape parental authority and, after interviewing successfully for various jobs in

London and rejecting them, I eventually secured a post in Devon. My parents found me a basement flat in a block of beautiful Georgian apartments known as The Crescent. Sharing with a young woman whose father, a medical consultant, ran a private practice in the apartment above, I was to live there during the week and return home at weekends. All seemed safe and above board. Except that it soon became clear that my flatmate had boyfriend problems and, being a diabetic, she attempted suicide by withholding her medication. The boyfriend, to the best of my knowledge, ran a mile and so began a series of male visitors making their presence known through the bedroom wall. This being the Sixties, such practice, I was told, was considered nothing more than female emancipation.

My job in the typing pool at the Legal & General insurance company, later at a firm of surveyors, and later still in the office of a large high-street department store, brought me in enough money (£17.00 a month) to pay my rent, contribute my pound a week for food, and my bus fare back and forth from home some twenty miles away. Somehow, in that first month, I managed to splurge the entire amount on a long black ball gown – typical of those on *Strictly* – and long evening gloves. Convincing myself that they were essential items of clothing, I wore them first to a naval function to which I'd been invited, and again to a dinner on board a British ship that had been purchased by the Indian navy. My first ever meeting with Indian officers and their wives, it was an experience I shall never forget, affirming as it did all my father had to say in favour of them.

Dances were held regularly at one of the local hotels and, given my parents' penchant for dancing, this became one of my favourite activities – ballroom and jive. Visits home held their attraction, too, as Clive, my parents' naval friend, was wont to throw wild barn dances at the farmhouse in which he lived. The West Country, in those days, was just beginning to become a haven for the wealthy and elite. When Clive sank his naval retirement fund into a property in town and opened a restaurant, he attracted just the sort of public school boys that my mother would have hoped for as a son-in-law.

Except that my flatmate's sexual behaviour was increasingly becoming the norm among my generation. By the time one of the public school boys fulfilled my mother's hopes, despite being still a teenager, I was already pregnant. Having failed my father's goals for me as an academic, my failure as a person of moral upstanding could not be more pronounced. When I left home, finally, to take up residence in Yorkshire, Dad wept openly. I suspect that the Lord, to whom I had made a commitment only a few years earlier, did so too.

Reflections & questions

The urge to leave the nest your parents have provided for you, is a natural instinct to adolescents. Although sad for those left behind, it allows the young the opportunity for a learning curve to take place. While steep to begin with, this ultimately brings with it the chance to be free; to be independent; to take responsibility. Unsurprisingly, there are risks. Watching an eagle step off a mountainside for the first time is enough to make any of us hold our breath. Will it catch the prevailing winds? Or will it crash to the ground? Will it find its way back? Or will it be swept away to oblivion?

The result, of course, owes much of its success to past and present. But not entirely. Maturity in human beings relies to a large extent on upbringing, but also on personality, attitude, circumstances and culture. Additionally, biological factors play their part. As the BBC programme *Child of Our Time* revealed, changes to the brain in adolescence mean we become more self-consciousness, and we are wired to feel pleasure more intensely than at any other time of our lives. Peer pressure, too, is shown to affect behaviour.

Just as no one knows for certain which of the scattered seed will come to fruition and which will perish on the way, neither can we predict the future for ourselves or our loved-ones. Yet, as I was to learn from my own life, there was the good and the bad: the seeds that took root, and the weeds that sought to choke them. I learned so much from Paul Gallico about the art of writing. Once again, my knowledge and understanding were acquired not by erudite means, but simply by assimilation. This, it seems, was the best means of education for me. The prevailing winds were in my favour.

When it came to personality and attitude, however, I failed dismally. While I have no wish to make excuses or pardon myself, I do wonder now whether the nightmare of my childhood, in which I looked down on my grave and wondered if my parents might now love me, was demonstrable evidence of the need within? Could it be that, like many young women today, it was this that drove me to seek love in the arms of any young man who showed interest in me? Or was I simply a child of my time?

Whatever the answer, there was good and bad to follow. While empty pursuits had robbed me of my new-found faith and left me with spiritual poverty, in God's hands those same events would lead me, ultimately, back to him. In the meantime, though, there was cursed ground, painful toil, and thorns and thistles to face.

'Because you listened to your wife and ate fruit from the tree about which I commanded you, "You must not eat from it," cursed is the ground because of you; through painful toil you will eat food from it all the days of your life. It will produce thorns and thistles for you, and you will eat the plants of the field.' (Genesis 3:17–18)

- What parental expectations do you feel were imposed upon you, if any? How did you deal with this, and was the outcome good or bad?
- If you are a parent, yourself, is this something you've considered when raising your children? Might it be something worth discussing with them?
- What about the culture of the times in which you grew up? Or your schooling? In what ways did these shape your life for better or worse?
- Did leaving the nest see you flying high, or falling to the ground?

GOD'S PURPOSE FOR US?
Like the Prodigal Son, we are to learn the lessons of profligacy and riotous living.

15: Pruned and Propagated

The eternal God is your refuge, and underneath are the everlasting arms. He will drive out your enemies before you, saying, 'Destroy them!'
(Deuteronomy 33:27)

The thing I loved most about James was his vulnerability. And, of course, the Pied Piper qualities beneath which it was hidden. He was the initiator, the organiser, the trailblazer of all that took place, while others followed; not meekly, but galvanised and filled with his enthusiasm. It was he who decided the when and the where of all social events with our friends: which pub we should frequent, where we would eat, which beach would host our barbecue. And off we'd go, a fleet of cars, a flotilla of small boats, a flock of sheep following, though not ostensibly herded.

We first met through Clive, my parents' naval friend: the party-thrower. It was my exceptionally long scarlet fingernails that attracted James, so he told me later. As for me, I fell in love there and then and, despite the heartache of the years that followed, in effect I never really fell out. Fortified with booze, I was as enthusiastic a follower of the Pied Piper as anyone else. Introvert or not, fuelled with alcohol I could match any extrovert pursuit.

James' gregarious nature was a magnet. But so, too – at least to me – was his little-boy-lost appeal. Dark-haired and good-looking he might be, but he was far from being the epitome of manhood. Lacking height and stature, his chief failing – or so it seemed at the time – was his stutter. And it was this that signalled his greatest charm as far as I was concerned. A cause of embarrassment to his followers, to me it brought out all my mothering instincts: patience, kindness, a listening ear, encouragement. My attention was thus redirected – away from the irredeemable infallibility of my own failings, towards one whose imperfections I hoped I might help to rectify. Or at least placate.

Sadly, my love for James was not entirely reciprocated. That much he made clear from the start. He did not want to father a child. I wept. But with the clarity born of my father's influence in perceiving all sides of an argument, I was able to see where he was coming from. So if he didn't want to marry me, I'd go it alone, I told him. And I meant it, though quite how I would have managed I have no idea!

We married. We moved to the north of England where James worked in his family business, and rented a flat. With no motorways, no internet, and only expensive trunk calls to be made on a landline, it was a long way from home and I missed my parents hugely. God provided, however, with a kind and helpful landlady, plus James' grandmother. A lovely hospitable woman who knew the Christian name and circumstances of every employee in the family firm, she became a surrogate mother to me. And, with a faith of her own, a huge Christian influence in my life.

To date, despite the Bible I'd been given as a nine-year-old by my aunt, my attendance at Sunday school throughout my childhood, and the commitment I'd made as a fourteen-year-old, my faith had not developed in any meaningful manner. The seeds God had scattered and nurtured in my life remained immature, belief in him being the object of my focus, rather than discipleship about which I knew little or nothing. *You can believe and pray to God in a field,* I repeatedly told myself and others; *there's no need to go to church.* Thus, still lacking in confidence, I revelled in the lifestyle afforded by my new husband and, with enough booze inside me to quell my sense of inferiority and inadequacy, I more than coped with the pubbing, the partying and the profligacy.

Following surgery, because the complicated nature of my innards had caused my pelvis and womb to tilt, our first child was born. The miracle of motherhood engulfed me as I held her, thrilled with the perfection of her tiny hands and pearl-like fingernails, the curling lashes on her rosy cheeks. To think that this beautiful little being, created by God, had grown within me! More than that, he'd ensured that I'd only taken a few of the Thalidomide pills I'd been prescribed for morning sickness – now shown to have caused terrible deformities in so many children of that era – and that they had had no effect on my baby. How could I not feel overwhelmed? Sarah, with her smiley little face, continued to delight us all.

The daily ordeal of having to hand-wash all the nappies and baby garments, along with scrubbing the blackened collars of seven shirts a week, was a stark contrast. Since the London smog of 1952, in which we had all been compelled to wear masks to school and 12,000 people had died, a Clean Air Act had been brought in, but this was not applied outside the capital until 1968. Carting the washing downstairs to be hung on the line in the backyard or putting the baby out in her pram, I would be greeted, within an hour, by the results of the pollution: black-spotted laundry, and the white outline of the baby surrounded by sooty deposits.

When a second pregnancy occurred, it became clear that the flat was no longer suitable. With financial support from James' grandmother, a large house was purchased in a relatively wealthy area of the city, which we promptly converted into three flats in order to give us extra income to repay the loan. Like the Surrey property purchased by my parents, our new home had once been owned by a doctor who had used it as his surgery. Our ground-floor accommodation was, therefore, certainly not lacking in size. Outside, in the walled garden, stood a series of outhouses, one of which became a utility room housing – miracle of miracles – a newly-purchased washing machine.

With my twenty-first birthday due soon after we moved in and most of the building work completed, we had sufficient space for a number of hired trestle tables to be set up in the sitting room, and I cooked a meal for a couple of dozen of our friends to celebrate the occasion. Other than an unfortunate occurrence in which the baby's pram blew upside down, with her in it, the event was a huge success.

Happily, the pram landed right over a trench dug by the builders to house the water supply and drainage for the new bathroom, so she was unhurt.

Victoria's birth, only thirteen months after Sarah's, was, once again, not without difficulty due to my intestinal problems. As both took place in a local private nursing home run by nuns, I was well looked after and returned home none the worse for wear. I adored them both, as I did their father. I breastfed my babies, sang to them and read stories to them. All my artistic instincts came to the fore as I knitted and sewed little garments for them, using my skills in embroidery and smocking. As they grew older, I delighted in teaching them: to read a recipe; to weigh and measure; to make cakes and doll's clothes. In all respects, motherhood was exactly what I'd hoped for and imagined.

To begin with, James made it clear that he expected me to continue with the pubbing and partying but, eventually, motherhood somewhat curtailed this for me. That was no great problem from my point of view. Except that I saw less and less of him. Giving the excuse that he was working late, he would return home inebriated more and more frequently. When we acquired a black Labrador puppy, following a trip to Settle, in North Yorkshire, 'walking the dog' became the excuse for a visit to the local pub. Named Samantha, after a TV drama, she even had her own ashtray as a repository for a drink of water with an occasional dash of beer.

Then one day, having had to consult my doctor for gynaecological problems, I was told I would have to visit an STD (Sexually Transmitted Diseases) clinic and, because of the nature of the disease, my husband would have to be informed. With which I learned that he had picked up the infection from a prostitute – a one-off, he assured me. It was devastating, but I had no choice but to believe him.

Our marriage might not be what I'd hoped for but, despite the lack of time spent with James, I managed to make a life of sorts. With a local shopping centre down the hill and a park at the end of the road, it couldn't have been easier to sit Sarah on the end of the pram, put the dog on the lead and take them all out. Besides, because of James' family connections, I'd made some good friends and, being the only one who was married and had experienced the joys and woes of pregnancy and labour, I was once again the focus of attention. Life couldn't have been better.

At least, until our eldest was two-and-a-half.

I'd had the flu, and no sooner had I recovered than Sarah fell sick. It soon became clear that her ailment was more serious than mere influenza. I rang for the doctor and was told a locum would have to attend but, as the snow lay thick on the ground, his arrival might be delayed. Frantic with worry, I paced the floor throwing little arrow prayers to God for her recovery. The doctor arrived in due course, took one look at my infant daughter and rang for an ambulance. Making some sort of provision for Vicky's care, I followed it down to the children's hospital and stayed while she was admitted.

Returning home after collecting Vicky, I opened the front door and thought the hall ceiling had fallen down. The floor was covered with small white pieces of litter. Our lovely black Labrador puppy slunk towards me, tail between her legs. And then I realised! Clearly, bored out of her mind, Samantha had found one of the children's stuffed toys, a gonk (the 1960's equivalent of today's minions) and chewed it to pieces. Not only that, she'd found a bag of light bulbs and demolished them! As if one sick child wasn't enough, I was now faced with the prospect of a sick dog.

Sarah, we were told over the next few days as lumber punctures were carried out, had encephalitis, a complex and severe condition in which inflammation of the brain tissue causes its dysfunction. She might recover or she might not. And if she did, it was highly likely that she would be brain damaged and physically disabled.

My pleas to God ceased to be arrow prayers shot randomly into the dark, and became earnest petitions to my heavenly Father. Turning to the Bible Auntie Phyl had given me for my ninth birthday, I devoured what it had to tell me. How could I lose the daughter I loved so dearly? The baby the Father had knit together in my womb and known before she was born? The child he'd so fearfully and wonderfully made? (Psalm 139:13–14).

Vicky, still only a year and a half old, had to be cared for while I made daily visits to the hospital and the only option, it seemed, was to send her hundreds of miles away to my parents in Devon. It was to be a decision I was to question daily in years to come, but at the time there seemed no alternative. Visiting daily, and with Sarah in a coma in a side room, I began to read stories to the other children on the ward. The trauma intensified. Brain damaged or not, I did not want to lose my darling daughter. Separated from both my children, I pleaded with God for their safe return.

'If you will allow Sarah to live,' I prayed, 'then even if she is physically disabled, I will bring her up to know and love you.'

Weeks passed. Months even. But eventually my prayers were heard. Sarah returned home as alert and active as ever, and our family was intact, once again. What's more, only two years later she passed the entrance exam for the local Public High School for Girls and, among hundreds of hopefuls, secured one of only two places available. It was, I thought, as if God wanted to assure me of his power and might.

Somehow, during Sarah's illness, news of our plight filtered through to the local vicar who, it transpired, lived only three houses away from us. Another God-incident? Certainly the Gardener's intervention in pruning and propagating what had emerged from the seeds he'd planted in my life. Calling one evening before James had returned from work, Revd Michael Cole offered to pray for us as a family, and invited us to church. Was this, then, to be the turning point for me?

Reflections & questions
Despite my immoral behaviour which had led to the less than desirable circumstances of my marriage, God's intervention and protection was palpable on no fewer than three occasions. I'd refused

to terminate my pregnancy (illegal until David Steel's Abortion Act in 1967), but might well have lost my baby when surgery was required before her birth. God decided otherwise. Had I then continued with the course of Thalidomide that had been prescribed to me for morning sickness, who knows what effect it might have had on my child? God protected her. And while there are those who might disclaim these incidents as pure chance, Sarah's recovery from encephalitis, which might either have killed her or maimed her for life, must surely be proof that the Lord had never deserted me or my child; that on the contrary, his loving arms were beneath us and around us; that the enemy who sought our destruction was, himself, destroyed.

I can't pretend to have been a perfect mother, however. Still needy, myself – particularly after the devastating revelation of James' liaison with a prostitute – I'd sought his attention by attempting to continue with his lifestyle, pubbing and partying to the undeniable detriment of my children. Yet again, though, God's hand was upon us! Unable to keep up with James' way of life when Sarah was in hospital, I was provided, instead, with the opportunity of rekindling and nourishing my faith. With the arrival of Michael and Stephanie Cole in my life, fresh growth and new shoots were about to emerge. Like a tree that was cut down, my faith was to sprout again.

At least there is hope for a tree: If it is cut down, it will sprout again, and its new shoots will not fail. Its roots may grow old in the ground and its stump die in the soil, yet at the scent of water it will bud and put forth shoots like a plant.
(Job 14:7–9)

- What actions or irresponsible behaviour of yours, if any, has thwarted your commitment to God?
- How, if at all, has this been redeemed?
- With women seeking equality with men, do you think the role of motherhood has been undervalued in recent times? If so, how might we restore it?
- If you are in the midst of difficult times, are you able to trust in the verses above which speak of the cutting down of a tree – in other words, being pruned?
- Do you believe that even when your hopes and dreams are cut back, if watered and nourished by God, they will shoot again? What experience, if any, do you have of this?

GOD'S PURPOSE FOR US?
To teach us that he is our strength and refuge.

16: Bearing Berries

And we know that in all things God works for the good of those who
love him, who have been called according to his purpose.
(Romans 8:28)

At twenty-three years of age, true to my promise to God made
nine years earlier, I began to attend church on a regular basis plus
Bible Study at the vicarage. Michael Cole, it seemed, had a rare
insight into the problems and frailties of my life. A fly on the wall?
As he preached, I felt as if he could read my every thought; see my
every action; hear every word I spoke. My sins, like weeds dug from
the ground, were laid before me on a regular basis so that I might
recognise and repent of them. My love for the Lord, nurtured and
cultivated by Michael's insight, developed and grew. Reaching for
the Son-light, my trust in the Father's goodness and faithfulness
grew taller and flourished. The seeds sown and grown in infancy
began to bear fruit in adulthood.

Meanwhile, Michael's wife, Stephanie, and I became firm friends.
With children of a similar age, we shared the highs and lows of
our lives unstintingly and without inhibition. Sewing and baking
together, attending evening classes in lampshade-making and
antiques, taking our children to the play-park or Botanical Gardens,
our faith in the Lord was paramount. Where once my neediness
of James' love had dominated my marriage, our relationship now
became a little more balanced. At least as far as I was concerned.

The American evangelist, Billy Graham, was due to visit that year.
When asked by Stephanie if I would like to attend the event, I was
more than willing. His preaching was inspiring, his faith dazzling,
his call to commitment inescapable. At least for others, yet not for
me. For when it came to participating as one of the hundreds moving

forward, I froze. Victim of my inhibitions, my claustrophobia, my fear of extrovert activity, I begged to go home.

You might think that the seeds God had scattered and nurtured in my life were about to become extinct. Not at all. When Stephanie asked me to go again to hear Billy Graham, this time in Leeds, where her parents lived, the Gardener ensured germination. Accompanied by my best friend, I answered the call to commitment, went forward, and received a blessing.

Naturally, a further call followed when Michael asked me if I'd like to be confirmed. With his teaching in church and weekly Bible studies at the vicarage, plus conversation with Stephanie, my faith had flourished. Knowing Jesus as my Saviour and Lord, conscious of the forgiveness his grace brought for past sins and those yet to be committed, plus the assurance of his presence in my life as my friend and guide, how could I not want to follow him? So now, aged twenty-five and six months pregnant with my third child, I made my vows and received all that Christ had to offer.

Sadly, James would have none of it.

'Why would I need God? I have everything I want,' he would say. 'Religion is for people who need a crutch. And I'm not one of them!'

We moved house, soon afterwards, only a short distance from our previous abode but into a far wealthier area. Selling the previous property, which we'd converted into three flats, we now occupied a large four-bedroomed detached property, with considerable garden space at the rear. Plus a huge mortgage to boot!

The move was necessitated by an increase in the family. A few years after Vicky's birth, I'd been hospitalised, yet again; not, on this occasion with back or intestinal problems, but with an ectopic pregnancy. This occurs when the egg is fertilised outside the womb and, before the days of keyhole surgery, yet another operation was necessary. Once I'd recovered, I'd then suffered a miscarriage. Convinced that the latter was due to my constant purging, and desperate for a third baby, three months into my next pregnancy I ceased taking all laxatives. Gestation continued uninterrupted but with no bowel movement for over a month I was in considerable pain and, once again, had to be taken into hospital for treatment.

Eventually, delivered by Father Christmas (he did his round of the ward while I was in labour), my third daughter was born in the convent nursing home where her sisters had come into the world, a precious addition to the family. With Stephanie's and my eldest daughters now at the High School together, our friendship remained intact. In due course, I became godmother to Stephanie's youngest son and she to my youngest daughter. However, despite the bonds, or perhaps because of their strength, I decided that I should support my local parish church. Sadly, probably because I'd acted without prayer, it proved to be an ill-judged move.

Unlike St Thomas's Church, All Saints seemed to be something of a misnomer. Even a whimper from an infant during the service brought frowns from the congregation. Consequently, I spent much of my time walking up and down the graveyard with Ruth in my arms. Nevertheless, when asked by the vicar if I would open my home for a Lent Bible Study I was more than willing, and subsequently perceived an invitation to join the Social Committee as the icing on the cake. Living, as we were now, in an elite area of the city, I knew the church's annual garden party was an event not to be missed. Clearly, I hadn't reckoned on what was to come. Meeting with the committee, I learned the real state of affairs.

The name of a well-known overseas missionary society was put forward as the possible recipient of the funds that would be raised.

'The children in that country have never heard of the gospel and they are desperately short of Bibles,' said one well-meaning lady.

'Why send it to people we don't know,' said another, 'when we could spend it on landscaping the church grounds?'

The debate that followed disgusted me and, when a resolution for the money to be spent in this way was passed, I resigned from the committee, and returned to Michael Cole's church once more.

The arguments were similar to those I heard, repeatedly, from my husband. When I asked for an allowance, reluctantly admitting to wanting to be able to give a tithe to the church, I was told that the church's wealth was deep and wide. What I didn't know was that our own income was now little more than a trickle. Nor that it was about to become a drought.

It all came to light late one evening when James was delivered home by friends in a worse state than usual. After a good deal of persuasion on my part, I learned that he'd fallen out with his uncle who ran the family business, and had lost his job. Worse still, he'd run up huge debts, and overnight it seemed that we were to be transformed from 'millionaires' to 'paupers'.

With three small children, a large mortgage, school fees, wages for our au pair and daily help (both necessitated by my ongoing health problems and hospitalisation), it was not a happy state of affairs. But it wasn't simply the money. James, immensely popular among his friends, had a vulnerability it seemed only I could see. Jokingly, in public, he would announce his qualifications as an FLC: 'Failed Loughborough College'. In truth, he was an excellent engineer but, when compared to his older brother who had science degrees at Cambridge University, he perceived himself as a failure generally, and a huge disappointment to his parents. That much we had in common.

It seemed natural, therefore, that when James proposed starting his own business, I should encourage him in his new venture. Securing further loans from the bank, he knew exactly what he wanted to do. So when my sister, Gilly, agreed to move into our home to oversee things, together with our Spanish au pair, Josephine, and aided by my lovely Yorkshire daily help, Mrs Higginbottom, I set off with James bound for America on what he called an 'industrial spying trip'.

Never one to do anything by halves, James ensured that we flew first class and had a suite in the Waldorf Astoria Hotel in Manhattan. This was my first visit to New York, so the usual sightseeing was a must: the Empire State Building, Statue of Liberty and Central Park. James had also planned a trip to the theatre on Broadway to see *Chicago*, a raunchy musical which left me squirming.

A few days later, he left early one morning bound for Boston where he had a business meeting. This being the first time I would ever have flown alone, I had strict instructions as to which flight to take to join him later in the day. In the event, some sort of emergency occurred and, instead of flying out from JFK airport, I had to take the shuttle flight to La Guardia and fly from there. This being before the advent of mobile phones, I had no way of alerting James and, on arrival in Boston, I found no sign of him. After several frantic hours, I learned that his plane had been unable to touch down due to adverse weather conditions, and he'd had to take the next step of our journey without me. The result was that I had to fly to Los Angeles alone, a terrifying experience given that it was a longer flight than crossing the Atlantic, and that all passengers had to remain strapped in throughout because of electrical storms and extreme turbulence.

The result of the business trip was rather better. A trip to France followed. Being fluent in the language, having lived and worked in Nantes, I was to act as interpreter. Following visits to various French steel-cutting factories, further trips took place, notably to Hong Kong, where my uncle worked for the government, then to Australia and Japan. Until, at last, the way ahead looked clear.

Having completed his research with me in tow, James eventually purchased a laser cutter. The first ever to be brought into the UK, he mounted it on a Plessey profile cutter and the new business was born. With both plasma and laser cutting, his innovative, entrepreneurial nature came to the fore. A failure he might feel by comparison to his brother, but his business was a huge success.

Sadly, it had the opposite effect on our marriage. With both his parents having been heavy drinkers, James had learned by example. Rarely out of the pub, he continued to roll home at all hours of the evening. Alcohol became the panacea for all ills: the escape from the wife with whom he'd no wish to spend any time, and the morality she now – perhaps hypocritically – attempted to present.

'We shouldn't really be doing this, it's illegal,' I'd say when, having been out for dinner with friends, James would pay the entire bill on his company card, collect cash from the other diners, and put the total down to company expenses in order to offset against tax.

'What's the point of paying accountants if you don't use the b***dy loopholes?' he'd respond.

Then there was the pay differential I discovered when working on the company accounts, for employees who were expected to be on the job all hours.

'How can they make a living?' I would ask, pleading with him to listen.

'They're lucky to have a b***dy job,' was his reply. 'And they have me to thank. Without my input of skills and finance, they'd be on the dole.'

I couldn't fault him there! But neither could I turn a blind eye.

From the outside, we appeared to have an idyllic lifestyle. James' popularity ensured regular social activity, with country walks, barbecues, parties and pub tours the norm. I, like my mother, took on the role of being hostess, entertaining clients, cooking, feeding and giving overnight hospitality to all who came to our house.

The only flaw, it seemed, were my ongoing health problems. If I wasn't on traction in hospital because of a slipped disc, or under the knife with some gynaecological problem or other, I had my intestinal issues to contend with. Dogged with pain and sickness, it was a closely guarded secret. I was too ashamed to admit to it, especially as no one in the medical profession had any answers for my complaint, other than that it was down to me: to take more laxatives; eat more greens; take more exercise.

If only!

James, meanwhile, was more than willing for me to take the children down to my parents during the holidays. Once there, we were spoiled and indulged by a loving grandma and grandpa. With the beach at the bottom of the garden and my youngest sister only five years older than Sarah, it was time well spent. Or so I thought.

Returning from a half-term visit to my parents, James' motive in encouraging me to go away so often became glaringly obvious.

Beneath my pillow I discovered another woman's nightdress. Stained and crumpled, it had clearly been worn. My stomach turned. Bad enough to imagine your husband's infidelity. Worse still in your own bed.

Reflections & questions
Being unequally yoked in marriage is denounced in Scripture:

> *Do not be yoked together with unbelievers. For what do righteousness and wickedness have in common? Or what fellowship can light have with darkness?* (2 Corinthians 6:14). *What harmony is there,* it continues; *or what does a believer have in common with an unbeliever?*

This was an issue that was very clear in my marriage. Yet, as far as I could see, I was to blame for it having occurred in the first place. The profligate and immoral lifestyle that had brought us together was not only that of an unbeliever, it was also alien to what little I knew of faith and to the upbringing I'd known at the hands of my parents. In all respects, I had failed!

Nevertheless, my hope when God brought me back to faith was that James, too, might begin a relationship with our Lord and find salvation and redemption. In reality, the opposite occurred. My new-found relationship with Christ was perceived as a sign of weakness and my encouragement for James to join me as flawed. In applying the adage of being unequally yoked by finding pursuits other than pubbing and partying for myself, I earned only his wrath. My gentle rebuke for financial wrongdoings was perceived as inflammatory. And in every respect, my prayers for my husband, undertaken in privacy as well as with Michael and Stephanie, appeared to fall on deaf ears.

As far as I can see, in a situation like this there is no easy answer. Remaining silent means being caught up in a lifestyle that is unconducive with faith. As is walking out! Being of one flesh, we're told not to separate that which God has joined together. Which is why the truth of Romans 8:28 became so relevant in my life. My persistent hope was that the way in which God had worked all things together for good in the matter of Sarah's health, and in James' business, was only the beginning. As far as I could see, there was nothing more I could do to further the hope of eternal life for James, other than to remain as one with him.

So neither the one who plants nor the one who waters is anything, but only God, who makes things grow. The one who plants and the one who waters have one purpose, and they will each be rewarded according to their own labour. For we are fellow workers in God's service; you are God's field, God's building. (1 Corinthians 3:7–9)

- What was the turning point in your making a commitment to follow Jesus and were other people instrumental in bringing that about?
- Did it involve some traumatic event like the near death of my daughter, or infidelity on the part of your spouse? In which case, could you vouch for the scripture that states 'that in all things God works for the good of those who love him'?
- What are your views on being unequally yoked – in marriage, or in business – and how should a believer respond to practices that are alien to faith?

GOD'S PURPOSE FOR US?
We are to stand firm in the faith; to be courageous and strong, in the knowledge that God has plans for our future.

17: Roots in Rocky Places

We know that suffering produces perseverance; perseverance,
character; and character, hope. And hope does not put us to shame,
because God's love has been poured out into our hearts through the
Holy Spirit, who has been given to us.
(Romans 5:3–5)

Was I stupid to accept the excuse James made about his secretary having had to stay overnight while he'd slept downstairs? Of course I was! Was I hurt? Desperately! Were there shouting matches? You bet! But as usual, it seemed easier to accept than to take action. True to my nomenclature, I saw myself as deficient. Who could blame him for seeking female company elsewhere when I was so often unwell? Thus was my reasoning. Failed as a daughter, I wrote in my journal; failed as a wife; failed as a mother. I was to add to that list in the years to come. And given that I was clearly wanting, what more could I do but accede to the status quo. Besides, wasn't that what the Bible told me to do? To ignore the speck of sawdust in my husband's eye while harbouring a plank in my own. To forgive. And so to forget?

They say opposites attract and that had clearly been true of James and me when we met. His extrovert nature had been like a magnet to me, allowing me a chance to shine despite my inferiority complex and natural instinct to bury myself in a book. Likewise, my deference and adulation for James had been the attraction for him. The problem now, it seemed, was the emerging of aspects of our lives that were clearly contradictory. And they weren't, always, simply matters of conscience and morality.

Having purchased our new home at an auction sale when I was heavily pregnant with Ruth (and under strict instruction from James who had been unable to attend), I had then set-to furnishing it with second-hand purchases. Rediscovering the traits of frugality, of make-do-and-mend, with which I'd been raised, I took great delight in the creativity afforded me in making my own curtains, lampshades, embroidery and dressmaking. Equally gratifying was the admiration I received from friends. This, however, was anathema to James.

'For G**'s sake! I'm sick of seeing you sitting at that b***dy sewing machine all the time. Everything on your back, and the children's, is there by your efforts. Why can't you just be normal like most people?'

Confused as to what was 'normal', it took me a while to fathom his reasoning. Was his fury the result of my independence? Was it, I began to wonder, a perception of humiliation, in which the wearing of home-made clothes denoted inadequacy on his part? And if so, was I to be nothing more than a walking advertisement for his success? In which case, I needed to change my own perceptions.

Yet even here there seemed to be no pleasing him, since spending too much on clothing for myself and the children also incurred his wrath. Utterly bewildered, I retreated into myself, hardly daring to express an opinion; rarely able to make a decision.

My prayers for James' conversion were equally clandestine and full of doubt. Why couldn't God do something? What did he want of me? How should I behave? Lost in a maze of torment and confusion, I pleaded to know the way forward.

'Why can't I be the sort of wife the Bible says I should be?' I wept silently, night after night in bed.

'I see nothing wrong with our relationship,' was James' retort whenever I tried to open discussion to seek the way ahead.

Next thing, he'd be berating me for drinking too much and thus talking too much; for refusing to go to the pub; for being a 'wet blanket' if I did and asked for orange juice. We were, it seemed, caught in a vicious circle of swirling tides and threatening currents. When I begged him to seek help with me from Marriage Counselling, he refused.

'If you don't like it, you know what you can do,' became his answer for every row we had. What he meant, of course, was that I could leave.

Increasingly, having opened factories in other parts of the country, he was away overnight on business. Until one day, when he failed to turn up for an early evening event we'd arranged, I could take no more and told him so on his return later that evening.

Filled with a courage I didn't know I possessed, I packed my bag and, leaving the children in the care of our au pair, I booked into an hotel for the night. Our personas took a giant leap. Stumbling panic and pleading took control of James, while I became increasingly calm and collected. He whined excuses; I stuck to my guns. He begged me to rethink; I shook my head. He became defensive and self-pitying; I told him we couldn't maintain the status quo.

However, reluctant to quash what I began to see might be God's leading, I eventually gave in to his pleading and agreed to dine with him; to talk about the future. My wisdom proved to be flawed. After we'd eaten, fortified with yet more booze, James followed me up to my hotel room, grabbed me, shoved me against the wall, and began kissing and fondling me. Aroused because intimacy between us had not existed for so long, I felt my knees buckle as I responded. He thrust me to one side.

'I could have taken it if you'd pushed me away. You're so pathetic!'

Was the look of disgust on his face for me? Or himself? I felt utterly confused.

Eventually, it all came out. He'd been having an affair, he spat at me. For over a year. Didn't I know? Couldn't I tell? He turned away and left.

The person in question was James' secretary, a young woman to whom I'd shown comfort and support when her boyfriend had deserted her. She had even come to live with us for a few weeks while she sorted out alternative accommodation. And it was she, I took it, who had slept in my bed. Was this my reward for kindness? Numb with pain, I lay down on the hotel bed, fully clothed, and remained there till morning.

Kind friends saw me through that period, though I spoke of it to no one else. How would my parents have reacted? I hardly dared imagine. A short time later, James asked me to take him back and I did. Immediately, he tried to resume a sexual relationship with me. Filled with revulsion, I could not respond. Barely able to perform the demands of domestic and family needs, I felt like a robot. For three days, James left each morning and returned each evening. Then he failed to come home. For night after night, I waited. The children were silent, their frightened little faces frozen into immobility.

Then one evening, he rang.

'I've never loved you,' he bellowed down the phone. 'I want to be with Claire. Do you know what it's like to love someone and not to be with them?'

Did I know? Yes, I knew.

Time went by. Then James' attitude changed.

'Don't do anything.' He made it clear that he meant consulting a solicitor. 'I might want to come back, after all.'

Weeks passed. Weight dropped off me until I was nothing more than skin and bone. But still God sustained my spirit. Driving daily out to the moors after I'd taken the children to school, I drank in the craggy barrenness around me, restored by the silence of the skies, the emptiness of the windswept heather mounds, the beauty of God's creation. The chorus, *Turn your eyes upon Jesus,* rang through my head constantly, *Look full in his wonderful face. And the things of the earth will grow strangely dim, in the light of his glory and grace.*

Then one evening, friends took me out for a meal. Joined by others, I learned the reason for their kindness as they reminded each other, in barely audible whispers, that this would have been my tenth wedding anniversary. Nausea rose in my throat. Excusing myself, I made my way to the ladies' room and, as James appeared at the door of the restaurant, I felt the floor come up to meet me.

A long time later, I learned that a doctor had been summoned, and that I'd been diagnosed as being on the verge of a nervous breakdown. Medicated with pills of all colours and sizes, I ensured that my parents knew nothing other than that I was 'unwell'. My father's reaction would otherwise, I knew, be one of violent retaliation. And the fact was that I still loved my husband. When I was told to 'pull myself together' and to 'snap out of it' by some of James' friends, I wondered what, if anything, they knew of the distress of betrayal.

Then I felt guilty.

'How can I call myself a Christian yet be relying on all these pills?' I asked Stephanie. And deep within myself, the guilt of my past threatened to submerge all sense of the forgiveness to be found in Christ. As the reassurances offered by my best friend fell on deaf ears, I spent hours of my life on my knees in prayer.

James moved back in. In my heart I'd forgiven him, but nothing was the same. We were like strangers.

'You're not the person I married,' he complained. 'You're no fun anymore. That church means more to you than I do.'

All I longed for was to be the wife he wanted. Yet I seemed to fail at every turn. Straight sexual activity no longer seemed to please and finding pornographic magazines beneath the mattress one day, I confronted him with them, bellowing at him and pointing out the risk that the children might come across them. When I received the usual taunting response, 'if you don't like it, you know what you can do', I simply couldn't take any more.

'If that's what you want,' I began.

'Call yourself a Christian,' he said contemptuously.

As on previous occasions, he started to throttle me then belted me across the face with his fist. Battered and bleeding, I ran to the front door and, despite the freezing night-time temperatures in the middle of winter and being blinded by tears, raced up the road, then trudged out of town heading for my favourite place on the moors.

Knowing that the scene had been witnessed by my children and that this couldn't go on, my intention was to allow nature to take my life. But it seemed that God had other plans. Hours later, suffering from the cold and thus numb in body as well as in spirit, I was found by a friend, was taken to a place of safety and, eventually, was returned home.

Reflections & questions

Other seed fell among thorns, which grew up and choked the plants, so that they did not bear grain.

How, you might ask, could this be God's *purpose* for my life? For any woman's life? Could anyone, in all honesty, suggest that he *picks* his followers to suffer in this way? Was I to be like the seed sown in rocky places where, having heard the word of God with joy, I was found to have no root and fell away when faced with trials and tribulations? Or like that which fell among thorns only to be choked and useless?

It seems not. Because as we're reminded in Romans 8:35–39 (ESV):

Who shall separate us from the love of Christ? Shall tribulation, or distress, or persecution, or famine, or nakedness, or danger, or sword? . . . No . . . neither death nor life, nor angels nor rulers, nor things present nor things to come, nor powers, nor height, nor depth, nor anything else in all creation, will be able to separate us from the love of God in Christ Jesus our Lord.

The paradox of why abused wives remain with their husbands is well researched, and psychological studies show a shift in blame to be one of the major factors. If accused often enough of being in the wrong, it seems that the victim ultimately accepts culpability. Add to that the biblical statements on submissiveness, the one flesh of marriage, and the 'sinfulness' of divorce, and it's easy to see that no Christian woman would want to augment the guilt she's already taken upon herself.

Sadly, this is common practice. Yet it should not be. Yes, we are all sinners. But that does not mean we have to submit to abuse. The gift of salvation and redemption is available to us all. Victim and abuser.

By the time my relationship with James reached this stage, my dear friends, Michael and Stephanie, had moved to Manchester. But as she reminded me repeatedly:

'You've left your sin at the foot of the cross and it's been nailed on with Jesus. So stop trying to take it all back again.'

When I shared this at a recent Lent study, another friend, Dr Norman Doidge, commented thus.

'The problem is that sometimes we only Blu Tack our sin to the cross. And that makes it all too easy to take it back. But the fact is that God doesn't simply *forget* our sin. He *chooses* not to remember.'

And that, dear reader, is a truth worth hanging onto!

- Do you constantly wallow in the guilt of the past or do you truly know yourself to be forgiven? If so, how?
- What clashes of temperament in relationships have you ever experienced, that have made you question the way ahead, perhaps even to the point of suicide?
- What is your understanding of what it is to be a submissive wife?
- What suffering have you incurred to make your roots go deep; what perseverance, character and hope have you experienced as a result?

GOD'S PURPOSE FOR US?
Acknowledging the sin in our own lives and God's forgiveness of us, we are to forgive those who sin against us.

18: A Yield of Sorts

*So the L*ORD *God appointed a plant and it grew up over Jonah to be*
a shade over his head to deliver him from his discomfort. And Jonah
was extremely happy about the plant.
(Jonah 4:6 NASB)

Sometimes, following an episode of abuse, James would be tearful and apologetic. On one such occasion he put forward a suggestion that we move to Devon where my parents would be on hand to support me. It seemed to be a good idea, the more so when we purchased a large Victorian house with sea views and only a short distance from the beach by my parents' home. James set up an office in one of the stone-built outhouses, and equipped it with a huge fax machine with the idea that I would take my part in running the business. Happy to be involved in this way, I truly believed this would be the start of a new life – despite all that had gone before, much of which I deemed to lie at my door.

Foremost among my faults and frailties were my health problems. Unseen by friends and family, they were nevertheless always present. Vacations abroad were fun, but a change in diet seemed to trigger constant problems. It was bad enough when tummy ache or sickness got the better of me, but when that turned to intense pain in my upper abdomen and the vertigo that accompanied it, I was good for nothing.

At the end of a family holiday in Lanzarote one year, I ended up being taken in a wheelchair to board the plane that was to return us home. Writhing in agony, and almost unconscious throughout the flight, I was administered oxygen by one of the passengers who was a doctor, and only later learned that this meant none of the other passengers were permitted to smoke.

On arrival at Gatwick Airport, no one was allowed to disembark until their names and contact details had been taken in case I was found to have some tropical infection. This meant missed connections for some, and isolation and barrier nursing in hospital for me. Tests showed no evidence of disease and my condition was put down to colic, intensified by the air pressure in the cabin, a condition suffered by the Queen's cousin, Angus Ogilvy, in the same week.

James, meanwhile, had booked into an hotel with the children and, to their great delight when I was released, he chartered a small aircraft to take us back to Devon. What fun they had sitting in the pilot's seat on the runway, or watching out of the window as we took a detour and flew over our house on the way back to the airport.

The point is, my health issues impacted on the whole family, and they weren't confined to my intestines. Frequent back pain had me in a steel corset on more than one occasion, and unable to do much at times. Was it any wonder I felt guilty and indebted? I asked myself.

But the fact is that God used my infirmities for good and brought about growth in me.

For as the soil makes the young plant come up and a garden causes seeds to grow, so the Sovereign LORD will make righteousness and praise spring up before all nations.
(Isaiah 61:11)

With James now home only at the weekends, I resolved to make something of my life. Although not a fashionista in any way myself, I decided to enrol in a course for interior design. It was no lightweight pursuit! In addition to studying colour and spatial awareness, I had to learn how to draw architectural plans plus designs fit for submission to council planning committees, as well as artistic pencil drawings showing the intended result for clients. Copious essays on construction and design filled my days, and before long I was discovering gifts I never knew I possessed. Gifts that, years later, were to be used in diverse ways.

Meanwhile, the children and I continued to attend church, this having been one of my concerns before we'd left Yorkshire. Knowing the services to be pretty vacuous in comparison to those led by Michael Cole, I'd asked him, prior to our move, if he could put me in touch with anyone who shared my faith. As a result, I'd met up with Pauline Gates whose husband's family were the Gates of Cow & Gate baby milk. A lovely lady who, when she left the Exclusive Brethren Assembly in which she'd been brought up, displayed all the thrill of a child in finding that there were 'real live Christians outside the Brethren'. Through her, I met with other women whose faith was filled with life and joy, and joined a Bible Study led by Jo Law, the wife of the vicar in a nearby village. In years to come, Paul and Pauline Gates were to take me to Hildenborough Hall which was then run by Jen Rees Larcombe's parents. My faith deepened and life was good, though I still found myself unable to speak about my problems.

'I love being able to meet with the other women for Bible study,' I told Stephanie on the phone. 'But I hate the lunches that follow because everyone talks about personal matters.'

'That's what I'd enjoy most,' she told me.

Knowing Stephanie as I did, I knew that to be true. We'd shared deeply and openly one to one when together, but I cringed at the thought of doing so in a group.

Family life, now we were living in Devon, improved immensely. My parents were wonderfully supportive and the children had immense fun with them. When their father was home, picnics on Dartmoor or on the local beaches were a constant. And when Sarah joined Island Cruising Club and the yacht club, she discovered a love of sailing that was to see her participating on the Malcolm Miller, one of the Sail Training Ships, and racing dinghies at weekends.

Her love of the water ensured yet closer bonds with her father, especially when he purchased a motor boat. We also acquired the Dartmoor pony that had belonged to my youngest sister, Kat, though Sarah was the only one who enjoyed riding. Vicky found her own hobbies, her favourite being to help farming friends with lambing, at which point she vowed she was going to be a vet when she grew up. While Ruth, a little clown full of laughter, delighted in swimming with my mother, painting my father's toe nails, or competing with him to see who made the most crumbs at mealtimes, or unknown to me, skate boarding with friends down the hilly zig-zag road from our house to the beach and risking collision with oncoming vehicles!

Despite the pleasures, there were normal family disagreements. Sarah loved reading, a habit no doubt acquired when she was still in the womb and was a shelf for my books. This introvert behaviour meant that she often did not want to partake in some of her father's extrovert activities, and she thus became the butt of his wrath.

'Let her be,' I would plead with James, but to no avail.

Then, aware that I had little in common with Vicky now she was growing up and was no longer my little 'moon-face', I would beg him to spend more time with her.

'You're so alike, you two,' I'd say. 'Same sense of humour, and clowning around. She needs to know you love her.'

'*Too* alike,' he retorted. 'Infuriatingly so. Can't bear seeing myself in her.'

Saddened, I reflected on my middle daughter's life. She seemed always to be in trouble, as if being naughty were the only way open to her to be noticed. Lacking the academic achievement of her older sister, she appeared to lack, also, any interests that connected her with her siblings or parents.

The children, since our move, had been attending the local primary school. But as Sarah and Vicky approached the age at which they would need to go on to secondary schooling, James insisted that this should be a boarding school.

'I went to Sherborne,' he said, 'and it did me no harm. And I think nothing of the local state schools.'

He was right in that respect. But having delighted in adding to my children's education by reading, cooking, sewing and gardening with them at home, I was very reluctant to have them disappear for an entire term. Feeling that they might benefit from weekly boarding, I proposed that as an alternative and a compromise was reached. It was not ideal because they fitted in with neither the day pupils nor the termly boarders, but they at least had the opportunity to enjoy all that their new home-town had to offer.

With fewer responsibilities now that it was only Ruth, the dog and me at home during the week, I was encouraged by my parents to join the local golf club and bridge club. Enthusiasts, themselves, they'd taught me how to play years earlier and felt it would do me good to follow my own pursuits. I never told them, but neither game was my forte. Lacking any form of competitiveness, I had no urge to win and, once again, I appeared to be a disappointment to them.

Nevertheless, it was a good way to become integrated in the community, I made some good friends, and it helped to pass what might, otherwise, have been a lonely week until James' return from work. Little did I know what was to come!

One Friday evening, returning later than usual because of the pressures of work and a difficult journey home, James professed to be in need of some shut-eye. While he went for a lie-down, I began to unpack his suitcase and sort out his papers as usual. Suddenly, unexpectedly, I came across some items which should not have been there. My heart raced. Clearly, I thought, like the nightdress under my pillow some years earlier, the sexy female lingerie amongst his washing must have been planted by the other woman in James' life. Perhaps in an attempt to force a decision in her favour? But what of the receipts for household items I didn't recognise – enough furniture to equip a home – plus an address of which I had no knowledge, and a life assurance made out in the name of his secretary? The woman to whom I had shown kindness and shelter in the past! Immediately, without saying a word, I stuffed it all back inside and closed the case.

Not wishing to create a to-do in front of the children, I waited until the following week when they were back at school and James had returned north. Tackling him over the phone, I learned that he had purchased an apartment, and had been living with his secretary ever since we'd moved to Devon. Was this, then, I asked, the purpose of our move?

James came home the following weekend and told me his affair was over. He no longer loved her. He loved me.

'She was pregnant,' he faltered, 'and had an abortion. I felt so guilty. I just couldn't live with myself if I abandoned her.'

My prayers that night, as on so many previous nights, revealed my sense of futility.

'Lord, bring my life to an end. Please! Take me to be with you. I want it to be over.'

Reflections & questions

You may, by now, be wondering why it was that I continued to live with my husband. I suspect that there may be an element of pity, or even disgust in the way you view me. It was once suggested to me that the affluent lifestyle James and I led might be the reason for my staying. That person clearly knew little or nothing about my values. Fear of the unknown was another reason put forward. Again, that was far from the truth, in that it simply didn't come into my thinking at this stage.

The truth was a complex amalgam: a spoonful of adhesion to the Biblical principles of marriage being for life; a sprinkling of forgiveness; a cupful of spiritual longing for James to come to know the Lord as I did; a large dollop of guilt and inability to forgive myself for past sins; and a pinch of justice in not wanting to condemn James when I knew myself to have been forgiven. Contained in a casserole of concern for my children's security and baked in an oven of my own ineptitudes, it rose to new heights each day.

In addition to the guilt, shame and humiliation cited as the reasons for women remaining in an abusive relationship, gratitude for kindness and clemency are said to be another explanation. Thus James' suggestion that we move to Devon to be near my parents was seen, by me, to be an act of thoughtfulness on his part.

Nevertheless, despite the fact that I felt utterly let down when I learned of James' betrayal, looking back I can see that there were benefits that came about because of our move. Learning to draw when I took up my interior design course was one, a gift that was to be used in the future. For the most part, though, I felt as Job had when a worm ate the shelter God had provided.

> *But God appointed a worm when dawn came the next day and it attacked the plant and it withered. When the sun came up God appointed a scorching east wind, and the sun beat down on Jonah's head so that he became faint and begged with all his soul to die, saying, 'Death is better to me than life.'*
> (Jonah 4:7–8 NASB)

- What gifts do you possess, which you discovered seemingly, purely by chance?
- What are the shared pursuits that bonded you with your parents; your children with you or your spouse?
- Have there ever been terrible secrets disclosed in your family? If so, how have they impacted on your life, and the lives of those you love?
- Have you ever felt, like Job, that God gave you a blessing – only to take it away later? If so, how did that make you feel?

GOD'S PURPOSE FOR US?
To trust the Light of the world, no matter how dark our days.

Reaping A Harvest
1976

19: A Harvest of Healing?

Those who sow with tears, will reap with songs of joy.
(Psalm 126:5)

Concerned for the security of my children, I took a firmer tone than hitherto, travelling north to consult my solicitor, a man of faith, whose advice was invaluable. Knowing where I stood, legally, gave me the confidence I'd previously lacked.

'I wish you'd been like this last time,' said James during one telephone conversation.

Aware of his contempt for me in the past, I wasn't surprised. My mind was clearer than it had been a year earlier, my life more independent since our move south, my ability to share my distress, to ask for prayer, now more mature.

'Trust in the Lord,' said Pauline Gates when I told her. 'And let the promises you read in the Bible drop eighteen inches – from head to heart.'

A font of memorable axioms, she helped me to deal with the feelings of jealousy and betrayal that besieged me.

'At least you're on the right track,' she said. 'Only main lines have tunnels.'

The explanation she gave revealed that it was only when we truly seek the will of God – in other words when we're on the main line – that we become aware of the darkness of our sin.

When anger and bitterness were a problem, she urged me to let go.

'Let the bad thoughts go through your mind. Through – and out the other side. Push them out with prayer.'

In the weeks that followed James' disclosure, I came to realise anew that God was at work in my life.

The books Pauline loaned me, particularly *Practising the Presence of God* by Brother Lawrence, brought clarity and perception to my understanding of the Father's word; a deeper and closer relationship with his Son. She introduced me to the minister who had recently taken over the local Baptist church. A lovely man, a real man of God, he in turn, introduced me to a young woman who had just miscarried and was on a search for God. Ill-equipped though I felt I was, it was in helping Lyn come to terms with her loss that I found my own comfort in the Lord.

Nevertheless, the strain of events had a profound effect on my health. When I slipped a disc one morning, reaching forward to pick something up from my daughter's bed, I found myself unable to move. Fortunately, someone called by and rang for the doctor who called an ambulance. The only good thing was that, with private health insurance, I wasn't being a strain on the National Health Service. Once again I was sent to the Nuffield and put on traction. With heavy weights tied to my ankles to stretch my spine, I was obliged to spend the next few weeks completely horizontal. And even when I returned home, once more, a steel corset was an obligatory item of clothing. A huge leather-bound metal device which stood more than a foot tall, I had no alternative but to wear maternity clothes to cover it.

As the weeks progressed and James and I were in touch more and more frequently, it became evident, eventually, that his affair was over and he wanted to come home.

'I never meant it to happen like this,' he told me.

And as he began to share his personal thoughts and feelings for the first time ever, so our relationship started to mend. No longer putting forward his desire to see the children as the sole reason for reconciliation, he began to court me.

'The first time we split up, I consulted a solicitor,' he told me, 'and realised I couldn't afford a divorce. This time, it's not finance that's the issue; it's the thought of losing you and the children.'

Once again I saw through the masque of leadership and business acumen that hid the little boy lost. Once again I saw the vulnerable child within the body of a man. Once again we attempted to make our marriage work.

My friendship with the Coles, meanwhile, had remained intact when they'd moved to Holy Trinity in Platt, Manchester some years earlier. Michael Cole had taken over from Michael Baughen, and I'd been to stay with them there on more than one occasion. Now, with another move and a new incumbency, they'd invited me to visit them in their new abode in Woodford Green.

I've always said that when God was handing out a sense of direction, I was looking the wrong way and failed to receive the gift. It was, therefore, with some trepidation that I set off. This being before the days of motorways, I took the A303 from Devon. Knowing I would have to traverse London, and wanting to avoid the Dartford Tunnel, I had no option but to take the North Circular.

'You did well to arrive so early,' Stephanie said to me as we hugged a greeting.

'I had someone sitting beside me, giving me instructions,' I replied, without thinking.

Puzzled, Stephanie frowned and shook her head.

'The Lord!' I responded. 'I wouldn't have had a clue how to get here otherwise. I just kept asking him: *Where do I go now?* Didn't go wrong once.'

It was true. It had come naturally to me to envisage my passenger seated at my side; to ask him for directions; to follow them without fault.

'You sound just like Corrie ten Boom,' Stephanie laughed.

At the end of my stay in the vicarage, she gave me a book. Titled *Nine O'Clock in the Morning* it was written by Rita and Dennis Bennet, and told the story of how baptism in the Holy Spirit had flooded the church in America.

'See what you make of it,' said my friend.

Returning to an empty house – James away at work, and the children at school – I immediately set to, reading about the phenomenon that had swept through the nation. Each night, thereafter, I prayed:

Please, Lord, let me be baptised in your Holy Spirit; let me speak in tongues; let me know your power and might in my life.

For three nights I prayed, thus. Then on the third night, 25th October, realising my fear and all that held me back, I told the Lord that I wanted to want him completely, but that only he could remove the blocks. *If it's not your will for me to be filled with your Holy Spirit – whatever you wish for me – I want only to be yours, completely and utterly.*

Nothing happened, and I fell asleep. Next morning I woke, full of joy, free of back pain, praising God, praying in tongues.

Two months later, on Christmas Eve, James arrived home from work and immediately wanted me to accompany him on a lunchtime drinking binge in the local pub.

'But what about the children?' I asked. 'They want to hang up their stockings. Write their letters to Father Christmas.'

'Oh, for G**'s sake! You always put the b***dy children before me,' he bellowed – not for the first time – and off he went.

Later that afternoon, I received a telephone call from a friend.

'I think I should warn you, Mel, James is in a bad way. He's in the pub mouthing off about some woman he's going to spend Christmas with.'

My heart stood still. When we rang off, I sat quietly in prayer. *Lord, I've asked you repeatedly to save my marriage, but the fact is that it's not MY marriage; it's YOURS.*

Recalling that, months later, it occurred to me that although God had honoured my pleas to save MY marriage over the years, this had not, necessarily, been for the best. If so, then in acknowledging HIS ownership of my marriage, had I, in effect, freed him to bring about his will?

At closing time that evening, when James staggered back home, a further phone call followed which I answered. It was Tony, James' best friend. He asked to speak to James and I handed over the telephone receiver. The conversation which ensued was one-sided and unheard by me. But I saw how James' face blanched.

'That was Tony,' he told me afterwards, as if I didn't know. 'He says that if I don't tell you, he will.'

'Tell me what?' I asked, my heart racing.

'I've been having an affair with Sheila,' he said. 'His wife.'

He buried his head in his hands.

Strangely, I felt only a sense of release.

Reflections & questions

Sometimes, it has to be said, we need the input of friends. Quite simply, we're not meant to go it alone. And that was exactly what I'd been doing for far too long. Brought up to believe the British stiff upper lip was unanimous with dignity and status, I'd allowed pride to dictate. Not wishing to be seen as weak or needy, I had barely shared my plight with others. But the truth was, that like Jesus in the Garden of Gethsemane, we need the prayerful support of friends.

Without the input of those we trust, we allow our minds to take control of us. And as Jeff Lucas, international author and speaker, wrote recently in *Life Every Day*, when we face difficult times, we need to give ourselves a good talking to rather than listening to a repetitive internal dialogue which is harmful. How right he was! Throughout my life my self-perception had been that of the 'naughty girl' and, in blaming myself for every negative event, I'd strengthened that viewpoint.

It was no coincidence that God had provided me with good friends like Stephanie Cole and Pauline Gates; nor that they had urged me to change my thinking; to understand and put my trust in what Jesus had done for me. *It is finished*, he said on the cross. And that's what we need to take on board. Our sin has been paid for. Completely. And forever!

Neither was it a coincidence that Stephanie had loaned me that book. The timing was perfect, as was the lesson God had set before me. I'd had to learn that prayer is not simply about *telling* God what we want and asking him to grant us our requests. We need to *listen* to him. To permit him to have his way in our lives. To submit to him. To allow him to fill us with his Holy Spirit.

Sometimes the result is that he will give us what we've asked for, as with my baptism in the Spirit. But sometimes, as I saw when I handed my marriage over to him, he knew that the best way forward for me was to end it. For only in pruning will the harvest be plentiful.

For, before the harvest, when the blossom is gone and the flower becomes a ripening grape, he will cut off the shoots with pruning knives, and cut down and take away the spreading branches. (Isaiah 18:5–6)

- Are you a loner, or do you have experience of the benefits of fellowship with God's family?
- How do you feel about sharing intimate needs? Does pride prevent your doing so?
- Have you ever been aware that you may know God as an honoured guest in your heart, but you've never actually handed over ownership of the property (yourself) to him? If so, is it now time to do so? Or are you held back by fear?
- How, if at all, has God used traumatic events to bring you to a deeper knowledge and love of him?

GOD'S PURPOSE FOR US?
To be filled to overflowing with the love, joy and power of the Holy Spirit, and to see God's will done on earth as in heaven.

20: Threshing the Grain

Grain must be ground to make bread; so one does not go on threshing it forever. The wheels of a threshing-cart may be rolled over it, but one does not use horses to grind grain.

(Isaiah 28:28)

It was late on Christmas Eve when I learned, without doubt, that my marriage was over. At the time, I felt a strange calm as if well prepared for the event. Looking back, I can see that this was, indeed, the case. I knew, with a quiet certainty, that my baptism in the Holy Spirit exactly two months earlier was no coincidence. Describing it, at the time, as having been the difference between inviting the Lord into my life as a guest in my 'home' when I first made a commitment and, ultimately, handing over ownership of the property (my heart and soul) to him, I could see for myself that he was now in control. This was clearly the case on Christmas Eve when, instead of praying for *my* marriage to be saved, I saw it as *his* marriage, and handed it over to God.

Nevertheless, the news James had given me was pretty devastating! He wanted a divorce. He was going to marry Sheila. Her husband – James' best friend, Tony – had lost both his parents that year, and he'd had to spend some considerable time abroad trying to sort out their business affairs. It seemed inconceivable that he should be betrayed in this way, by the two people closest to him.

Despite all previous occurrences, it still felt as if this was the first and I was numb with shock myself. However, there were other matters that required my urgent attention. The children, Sarah now fourteen, Vicky thirteen and Ruth nine years of age, were in bed and knew nothing of what was going on. We were due to spend Christmas Day at my parents' home, as usual. James – in no fit state to drive – was talking about leaving there and then. For everybody's sake, I asked him to stay and, when he refused, I rang his mother. Assuming that she would have some knowledge of the situation, I gave her the scantest of details and asked her to talk some sense into her son.

As a result, James stayed, sleeping overnight on the sofa. Next morning, at my insistence when he refused to spend Christmas Day with us, he told the children – in a sentence – that he was leaving me. Clutching their stockings from Father Christmas, the excitement and expectation on their faces evaporated to be replaced by tears and distress. Christmas Day passed in a daze.

Over the next few weeks, during which my parents gave me all the support I required, I consulted the same Christian solicitor who had advised me on previous occasions. James vacillated between wanting a divorce, then telling me we were rushing into it; saying what a fool he'd been and how lonely he was, then accusing me of holding things up; hurling verbal abuse at me one moment, then pleading for clemency in the next. My emotions followed suit: unimaginable hurt, followed by an inner peace; moments of hatred, followed by compassion and forgiveness. Thirsting for guidance, for healing, I turned again and again to my Bible, discovering the truth in the following verses.

And when they came to Marah, they could not drink of the waters of Marah, for they were bitter: therefore the name of it was called Marah. And the people murmured against Moses, saying, What shall we drink? And he cried unto the LORD; and the LORD showed him a tree, which when he had cast into the waters, the waters were made sweet.
(Exodus 15:23–25 KJV)

If you listen carefully to the LORD your God and do what is right in his eyes, if you pay attention to his commands and keep all his

decrees, I will not bring on you any of the diseases I brought on
the Egyptians, for I am the LORD, who heals you.
(Exodus 15:26)

I wish I could say I always listened and did what was right in God's eyes. I tried. But the truth was, stumbling through the desert that my life had become, I encountered many bitter waters in the months ahead. I wish I could tell you that the waters were sweetened, instantly, when I applied God's decrees. Or that I knew God's healing immediately. The reality was that hearing God's voice and being obedient to his commands was not a one-off. It had to be an ongoing, moment-by-moment situation.

Over the coming months, I discovered that James had run up huge debts with local suppliers and elsewhere. During the two years that it took for our divorce to be finalised, the question as to whether the children and I were to lose our home hovered over us like birds of prey. As did his attempt to take the children away from me by having our GP arrange for Vicky to see a psychiatrist who deemed that, because of my 'religious fanaticism', I was an unfit mother.

James insisted that many of the valuable antique items given to us by his grandmother had to be returned to him, though she put a stop to it when she realised he was selling them off to finance his new way of life. Meanwhile, he somehow put all his investments and assets in Sheila's name so that the children and I might have no claim on them. Then he purchased a motor boat gin palace.

Worse, was the impact on all those affected. Sheila and James lived together with her three boys, similar in age to my girls. Their father, Tony, hurt by the betrayal of his wife and best friend, suffered badly with depression. When I learned, later, that he'd been crushed to death as a result of having stepped between a truck – driven by a friend whom he was supposedly directing to reverse – and a trailer to which it was to be coupled, it fell to me to break the news to James.

Later, Vicky was suspended from school when she was found to be smoking, and a big question hung over whether it might have been cannabis. She then became entangled with a group of youths on motorbikes – one of them a doctor's son – who were eventually convicted of the gang-rape of a young woman on a nearby beach.

Sarah seemed the least affected though, being like me, I suspect that she hid her feelings well. Ruth, meanwhile, changed from being the bubbly bright little soul who brought smiles to all, into a little body in which the light had been snuffed out. James saw none of it.

The hearing for our divorce was traumatic. Ten men, including James, sat around a table discussing the possible future for the children and me, while I was made to sit at the other end of the courtroom out of earshot. One option put forward by James' legal team, I later learned, was whether my parents should be expected to house me so that he might sell our home. Given that my father's income was far less than my husband's, and that our residence was already in joint names at the insistence of my solicitor because of James' previous infidelities, I was appalled when this proposal was put to me. In the end, I was told that I might retain the house. But only with the encumbrance of a mortgage to be paid off.

At last it was over. Or so I thought. The truth was rather different.

Reflections & questions

It didn't take long for my friends and me to realise that James' vulnerability made him an easy prey for women. While I would not want to make assumptions, I can't think it was love or sexual activity he sought – he had both with me. Rather, I believe it to have been a need of unquestioning acceptance and admiration. And that, perhaps, was less evident in me once I'd made a commitment to the Lord. Certainly James would tell me, frequently, that the church was more important to me than he was. Could he have felt that my love for Jesus was a betrayal of our unity? Almost an infidelity? *Do not be yoked together with unbelievers* we are told in 2 Corinthians 6:14. But no one tells you how to deal with an existing marriage in which one becomes a believer and the other does not.

During our marriage I'd learned a fair amount about James' family life from his lovely maiden aunts. His older brother, it appeared, had shown exceptional merit in childhood. Lagging behind when out for a walk, he would be found, totally absorbed, examining the behaviour of insects. And it was this fascination that led to his becoming an entomologist.

I have no way of knowing for certain how this might have impacted on James as a small boy, nor how his parents reacted. Did they applaud their eldest to the detriment of his younger brother? Was their social life, which revolved around the golf course and bar, damaging to family time? Was it boarding school that instilled a sense of favouritism on the older brother and, thus, diminished the achievement of the younger? I don't know. I can only go on what I perceived. And that was the vulnerability hidden beneath James' outward behaviour. The whys and wherefores are beyond me.

It does make me wonder, though, if we, as parents, can ever get the balance right? I'm not advocating going over the top in praise. No child should grow up believing themselves to be the centre of the universe, or a little prince or princess. They need to understand that in the real world that will not augur them well. Merit has to be earned.

Nevertheless, each child needs to know they are precious and loved; and that their skills are recognised and applauded. And that, as I was to learn with one of mine, is not always easy. How do you encourage a child when you can't identify their strengths?

Whatever the reason for James' behaviour and my reaction to it, there's no doubt our marriage and divorce took its toll on our children. But, as the Bible reminds us, a certain amount of threshing is necessary if we're to be shaped as God wants us to be, and nothing goes on forever. That's easy to say in retrospect. Living through it is hard!

- What events have you been dreading for years which, when they at last occurred, brought you a modicum of peace?
- How have you seen God's hand in this?
- Using the analogy of throwing the tree into the waters, in what ways can you relate to your obedience to God having sweetened the bitter circumstances of your life?
- How, if at all, have you experienced or observed the effects of bad parenting skills?

GOD'S PURPOSE FOR US?
To show love and trust in the Lord in the midst of conflict.

21: Drought Followed by Fruitfulness

Don't judge each day by the harvest you reap but by the seeds that you plant.
(Robert Louis Stevenson)

Still in my early thirties when my divorce was finalised, it seemed to me that the social mores of the time made a divorced woman a pariah: no longer sociably acceptable at the dinner table with friends who'd remained as couples. Perhaps, even, a threat to their security? Equally, one became a target for single men; a temptation that I regret I eventually succumbed to.

The children, meanwhile, reacted in their own way. Ruth, still only ten years of age, continued to bottle everything up and, despite all my efforts to get her to talk, would tell me, midst her tears, that she didn't want to 'bother' me. Thinking back to one of the essays she'd written at primary school, in which *'I love my daddy; my daddy is lovely'* had figured repeatedly, it was not difficult to fathom what was going on in her mind. But how to heal it? That was beyond me.

Sarah, the eldest, became the little mother, particularly when the children visited their father. Helpful though this was intended to be, there was no doubt that it also engendered some resentment in the minds of her siblings. Her shared love of boating with her father, when he took them on his gin palace, was also divisive.

But it was Vicky's response that evoked the most concern. At some point when she was staying over with a friend in Plymouth, I received a phone call from the police in the middle of the night. Informing me that she'd been arrested for brawling, they told me I was to come immediately to collect her from the police station. With little alternative, I woke Sarah and left her in charge of Ruth until I returned from the fifty-mile round trip.

It was clear that Vicky's behaviour was a cry for attention; a hoped-for means of bringing her father and I together to sort out her mess. And when on leaving school she became increasingly involved in drugs and related activities this, indeed, was the result.

My parents were wonderfully supportive to me throughout and did all they could to ensure that my life, and the children's, was as full and happy as was possible. Having encouraged me to join the bridge club and golf club, both parents spent endless hours endeavouring to teach me the skills that were required to bring me to their level of success. Still eager for their affirmation, I did all I could to please. The truth was, though, that although I enjoyed the fresh air and beauty of our surroundings, plus the opportunity to offset loneliness with small group entertainment by playing bridge at home, I had no interest, whatsoever, in competitive games or sport.

Nevertheless, there were gains to be made spiritually. Over the years that followed my divorce, I was better able to see and evaluate the seeds that had been sown and grown in my infancy, and those that had put down roots and sent up shoots in my childhood. Some, like the love of parties, competitive games and sport that my mother tried to foster in me, had fallen on stony ground, to be pecked away, eventually, and seen no more. Others, choked out by the brambles and weeds of the adverse circumstances surrounding me during my married life, now seemed determined to survive and thrive strengthened, perhaps, by their enforced fight for survival. Rain aplenty had pelted down in the form of my health issues, but sunshine had also made itself known to me as I'd nurtured my children in the hope of seeing them bloom.

The seeds of faith, sown by God himself and tended by the loving hands of Michael and Stephanie Cole, Paul and Pauline Gates and others, had survived the soil and toil of life, and were now about to thrive. A leaf of belief had given way to buds and blossom, until now, with the grain matured and the fruit about to fall, harvest time had arrived. I began to recognise that I'd been picked for a purpose.

Perhaps because of my enthusiasm at church, I was asked to

become Sunday School Superintendent and to join the Parochial Church Council. Words fail me when it comes to describing the joy it brought me teaching the children about Jesus' love of them. But it was in seeing the bigger picture that I felt I really made my mark. Faith, in my view, was not simply about learning or worshipping on a Sunday: it was about being part of God's family and revering his creation every moment of every day. With the help of others, I arranged to take the children for outings – picnics, swimming, or dry-ice skating at the The Pavilion in Torquay – helping them to bond as they learned to share and support one another; highlighting for them the world that God had created.

The nativity, at Christmas, was no longer simply a display of figurines. The children, themselves, took part as angels, shepherds, Mary and Joseph, even, on one occasion accompanied by a real, live donkey! Having made its presence known by depositing a large and smelly pat of manure on the church aisle as it bore Mary (my daughter, Sarah) towards the chancel, however, I somehow doubt that it was ever asked again.

Then, in an effort to get to know the Sunday school children's parents, I arranged for a party. Held in the home of one of the PCC members, I recall the gaffe I made which, ironically, highlighted the need I was trying to address.

'John, let me introduce you,' I said to one parent. 'Have you met Sally before?'

The two exchanged a glance and a moment of silence ensued.

'I think so,' John replied with a smile, 'we share the same bed every night.'

Duh! I hadn't realised they were married.

Equally, there were things others had failed to realise. When I discovered at a PCC meeting that the church gave financial support to the Dame Hannah Rogers School – a home in Ivybridge for disabled children – I had a suggestion to make.

'It's all very well giving them money but what about getting to know them?' I asked.

And so, with clergy permission, I arranged that the children should be brought to church one Sunday morning for family worship, and would then go home with some of the Sunday school children – including my own – for the rest of the day.

The school mini-bus delivered the children and the service went well. But I'll never forget the look of horror and fear on the faces of the parents who'd agreed to take a child home with them. Some of the youngsters were in leg braces, some in wheelchairs, and others suffered from Downs' syndrome or had speech problems. Shooting an arrow prayer to the Lord, I asked him to make the most of the occasion.

And so he did! When we gathered before the church at the end of the day, the faces of parents and children were transformed. A sense of genuine love, joy and affection abounded. They had bonded with the disabled children for whom they'd cared that day. The occasion affirmed in one and all that the Kingdom of God is not simply something to be taught through words and worship; it is a sense of family, fun and friendship; an attitude of acceptance; and recognition that we are all made in the image of God.

Reflections & questions

Looking back on my divorce, I realise how little understanding there was from those who had never experienced the trauma of a marriage in which both are unequally yoked. That is not to say that they failed to show compassion. It was simply that they seemed unable to recognise the emotional impact. Some were of the opinion that repetition must lessen the distress.

'Surely it can't be so bad second or third time round?' I was asked, as if a breach in trust, unlike a broken leg, heals more rapidly and completely with each subsequent fracture.

The fact is, as a German research on pain perception concluded in the journal *Pain*:

While athletes showed increased pain tolerance, they didn't show any difference in pain threshold (the level of stimulus at which they start perceiving pain). In other words, it's not that athletes don't feel pain – they feel it the same as everyone else, but they've learned to cope with or ignore it.

But trust, if the marriage is to be mended, has to be restored and is just as painful, if not more so, when broken again. However horrifying the disaster one faces, or the dread of what the future might hold, the body's survival mechanism ensures a release of neurochemicals and hormones into the brain to see it through. In the midst of my divorce proceedings, this had been my experience. A sense of exhilaration, almost, in which I had felt lifted high, as in a hot air balloon. Adrenaline had become the oxygen that inflated the balloon; prayer and trust in God the wind that propelled it.

Unaware of these consequences at the time, the after-effect, I found, was devastating. God had journeyed with me through the events that had required my intervention during the divorce proceedings. But once it was over, it was as if he, like the hot air balloon, had drifted away, leaving me to my own devices. Crashing to earth and wallowing in a mire of solitude and emptiness, I had initially allowed myself to become a sitting target for morbid self-pity.

Until, that is, I'd realised the freedom my singleness afforded me in pursuing God's aims in my life.

But for what purpose are we picked, you might ask?

Continuing the farming/gardening analogy of the Bible, what God wants of us is to bear fruit or grain and thus nourish others; to grow branches to provide shelter for those in need; to sow seeds in their lives so that they, too, might grow and blossom.

Quite simply, God's purpose for each and every one of us is to convey the good news to others. And that is that he has a gift for us all; the gift of forgiveness and redemption from sin and, thus, eternal life with him thereafter. He has chosen us to be his messengers, to tell the world that if we are prepared to accept that gift then, through Jesus' life and death on this earth, we may all know salvation. Mercy and peace. Love and Joy. Light in the darkness of this world. We are to be envoys for the irrefutable fact that Jesus is the Way, the Truth and the Life. How we go about that, as I was to learn, depends entirely upon the gifts he's sown in the soil of our lives; those that have thrived and those that have died. The fruit we bear will thus be different for each of us.

- What difficult and traumatic events have you experienced in your life that have made you aware of God's presence journeying with you?
- How have you dealt with the times when he's seemed silent? Or absent?
- Have you been tempted by the lures of the world? Perhaps even succumbed to them? If so, do you know yourself to be forgiven?
- Have there been times when even Christian friends have appeared to be totally lacking in understanding? When they might, even, have been condemning of your situation? What response has that evoked in you?

GOD'S PURPOSE FOR US?
To recognise the seeds that have been sown and grown in our lives, and to make these gifts available to the Lord so that he might use the fruit we produce to nourish others and to sow seeds in their lives.

Ripe for Picking

1977–82

22: Re-Seeding

You did not choose me but I chose you, and appointed you that you
would go and bear fruit.
(John 15:16)

It was God's gift of creativity that most resonated with me. Having completed my course on interior design, I knew it was not for me. An introvert trying to impose her ideas on to others? Never! Nonetheless, I'd benefited enormously from what I'd learned, and recognised, once again, it was my affinity with words. My love of reading – seeds sown in early childhood – had grown into a love of writing plays and stories in my teens, though, other than one, written when I was fourteen, I'd taken it no further since then.

At that time, encouraged by my father who subscribed to *Argosy* magazine, home of H.E. Bates *The Darling Buds of May*, I'd submitted a ghost story I'd penned, in which the denouement showed the apparition to be that of a dog trapped in a cottage in the woods. Perhaps, had I stated my age, it might have been considered for publication. As it was, I'd acquired my first rejection slip and, other than journaling, had made no further attempt at writing. Now, with the understanding and recognition I'd acquired when writing essays for my interior design course, I resolved to start a postal course on creative writing.

Meanwhile, God, the Gardener, clearly had plans to further my resolution! Via a combination of gifting, friendship and circumstance, he began planting a seed-bed that was to lead to a field of wheat and, ultimately, to a harvest of grain that would feed others. It started with a letter I wrote to my best friend, Stephanie Cole, in which I shared, at length, the trauma of going through divorce.

The church is engaged in carrying out God's will in bringing the gospel to unbelievers and in relieving the suffering of the sick and poverty-stricken and lonely in the world, but it seems to me that ministering to the single parent is completely ignored, I wrote. *I have been staggered at how many Christian women (often in the infancy of their Christian lives, but some mature believers) . . . have indulged in an affair. . . Most have found, as I have, that their Christian friends, although concerned for them spiritually, have shown no understanding of the loneliness which, contrary to popular opinion, does not decrease with time . . . Invitations for a meal, a picnic, or pantomime . . . are seldom forthcoming from the busy Bible-studying, prayer-meeting Christians.*

'You should send this to the *Church of England Newspaper,*' Stephanie told me. 'Get it published!'

I have to thank my good friend for her persistence. When my piece was published, she urged me to continue writing, pointing out that there would be others in my situation and that sharing would help us all. How right she was! The letters I received from all over the world left me in no doubt of that. Speaking of the loneliness experienced by divorced believers, they pointed to the lack of empathy encountered in society. And the church!

I have read your letter . . . and never have I met someone who so deeply understands the situation of a Christian woman whose husband has left her, wrote one woman. *I endorse everything you have said.*

My divorce or the problems that go with it are never mentioned, said another. *The people of the church are far from me.*

I have not had any relationships with other men yet, but I, too, feel the longing to love someone and be loved in return.

And in yet another: *To throw Christ at me does me no good at all. My faith in him has not faltered but my faith in people sometimes is called into doubt.*

Having received one example of that, in letter form, I had every sympathy.

You probably feel like a captive . . . one woman wrote, condemningly,
*but really that captivity is in your attitude towards God. He wants you
to give up any thoughts of rights to this and that . . . so that you can be
satisfied only in him.*

Immediately, once I'd replied to each correspondent, I penned a
second letter to the newspaper pointing out that Jesus, himself, had
suffered the loneliness of solitude when his disciples fell asleep in
the Garden of Gethsemane and failed to support him in his hour of
need. No servant is greater than his master, (John 15:20) I finished.

The consequence of my letter-writing was that I began to see a
need, and to feel an urge, to reach out and help those whose shoes I
walked in. With long, lonely evenings to contend with, I had only the
company of my lovely, empathetic Labrador, who sensed my every
mood and would put her paw on my lap to comfort me whenever I
wept, which I did, frequently. So, with nothing to hinder me, I began
to write my memoirs, first in long-hand then transcribing my scrawl
by tapping away on the little old portable typewriter that had once
belonged to my mother.

'Send them to Derek Wood at Inter Varsity Press,' Stephanie
advised me during one of our frequent telephone conversations.

Derek made it clear from the start that my book was not suitable
for IVP publication, but he, too, exhorted me to continue and for
months, perhaps even years to come, he advised and encouraged
me. Even so, it was to be some time before I found success.

Meanwhile, at Pauline Gates' suggestion, I began to look into
starting a house group and, when it proved impossible to attract
sufficient people from the parish church, I opened it up to others.
Soon, a group of us from several denominations were meeting
together, sharing Bible readings and, crucially, how God's word
impacted upon our lives. Once again, I found the support I needed
and, I hope, gave back to others.

In order to give the children some sort of stability since their
father had left, I determined that we would remain in the family
home. With insufficient maintenance to pay off the mortgage with

which I'd been saddled, this meant I had to work full-time for a local estate agent until, eventually, taking the cue from my mother and grandmother's lives, I started up a Bed & Breakfast business with much success.

Now, nearly five years later, I became aware that it was time to move; to be replanted. Suffering from a lack of self-identification throughout my life, I felt I was fast transgressing from being nothing more than 'James' wife' back to being 'my parents' daughter'. Since reading *Nine O'Clock in the Morning*, which had brought me to the point of being Spirit-filled, I'd yearned for a charismatic form of worship to be the norm for me. At Stephanie's suggestion, I visited Guildford Baptist Church where David Pawson ministered. Sadly, with house prices way beyond my means, it was not on; but when I learned that Isca Fellowship had set up in Exeter, only a short distance away, it was a no-brainer. A so-called house-church because it had grown from meetings in people's homes, it now boasted a congregation of hundreds, all of whom worshipped regularly in a local school hall.

Now that Sarah was working in London, having completed her A-levels, and Vicky was living in Plymouth, James promptly stopped all maintenance payments to me. With insufficient money to pay the mortgage, and barely enough to meet council tax and utility bills, Ruth and I lived hand to mouth, making do on off-cuts from the butcher or learning how to make a chicken last the week. Unable to afford to heat the house, I found mould beginning to grow on the walls.

When I learned that Ruth's school fees had not been paid for the previous two terms and that she would no longer be permitted to attend as a weekly boarder, I had no option but to seek help and advice from Social Services. Reluctant to apply for benefits, as instructed by them, I wrote to my solicitor asking him to pursue the matter, and put my trust in God. I said nothing to anyone, save Stephanie, whom I asked for prayer.

In no time, cheques began to arrive in the post. First a refund for some forgotten purchase I'd made months earlier and returned because of a fault. Then gifts from people I'd never met nor heard of. People, I later learned, whom Stephanie had asked to pray for me. Their generosity and the provision of the Lord, was overwhelming.

Nevertheless, it was clear to me that a turning point had been reached. Our town, once a small fishing village, was fast becoming a fashionable and elite resort for second homes. Convinced that this was the right move, I decided to put my house on the market. It sold quite quickly, though the purchasers, knowing I was a single parent, betrayed me by dropping the agreed price by tens of thousands of pounds (more than five per cent) only days before exchange of contracts was due.

Having had my offer accepted on a more modest house in the outskirts of Exeter, I was hardly in a position to argue. But it hurt! As did the actual move: the wrench of leaving our lovely home had Ruth and me in tears. Nevertheless, driving over the hills en route for my new home, the beauty of the countryside, coast and Exe estuary spread before me, my heart lifted to new heights. I wish I could say the same for my parents who, I believe, saw my relocation as a betrayal to them. Despite this, they helped me move in and continued to be supportive.

Ruth's schooling, meanwhile, had been thoroughly disrupted. I'd had to pay a considerable sum for legal expenses in a fight for justice over James' non-payment of her school fees, had won the case, but got nowhere as he still failed to pay up. With limited funds, myself, I had no recourse but to enrol her in the nearby state school in Exeter.

But even here, God knew our needs. She immediately struck up a friendship with a fellow pupil whose parents were Christians. Not only that, I found myself living next door to a couple, my own age, who were believers. Worship at Isca Fellowship and attendance at the weekly house groups proved to be everything I'd hoped for. And with a new part-time job, working in the city centre as secretary to the director of a firm of estate agents, plus a day a week working in The Mustard Seed – a café and bookshop belonging to Isca – I was in my element.

Reflections & questions

Throughout the five years or so I'd lived alone since James' departure, the tension between spiritual and worldly life was marked. While my parents' help was laudable, being driven by loving kindness, it had the effect of binding me within the bonds of dutiful daughter. Equally, the loneliness and lack of identity that drove me into the arms of boyfriends, and the hope of love thereafter, reinforced the tug of war that had epitomised my marriage.

As Glynn Harrison writes in his book *A Better Story: God, Sex and Human Flourishing*, the sexual revolution of the 1960s and the radical individualism that followed, unravelled the concept of sexual pleasure being confined to the commitment of marriage. Putting this down largely to a) the economic changes brought in by the welfare state after World War II, and b) a second wave of feminism which brought about the model of gender equality and greater opportunities to women but undermined the need for a male breadwinner, he adds c) easier divorce and d) contraception as facilitating the liberalisation of sexual relationships.

As a single woman, I found myself a target for the attention of men. Sadly, while wishing only to maintain stability for my children and follow the way of Christ, I confess I fell prey to the culture of the times and the demands of my emotional and physical needs. Having written of this in my article for the *Church of England Newspaper*, I was surprised to find that there were Christians who endorsed this. While they stated that God would understand my need, I despised myself.

Convinced, at one point, that in pursuing a search for love I'd committed the unforgivable sin, of denying the presence of the Holy Spirit, I sought help in counselling. There I learned that there are no shades of grey in sin: all is black in the eyes of the Lord. And all, by his grace and death on the cross, is forgiven. Not only that, the fear and shame aroused by thoughts of having committed the unforgivable sin is, in itself, evidence of the fact that the Holy Spirit is still at work. It is he who brings us to repentance. And, no matter what our heart and mind might tell us, by laying our sin before God and nailing it to the cross, we are forgiven.

No one who is born of God will continue to sin, because God's seed remains in them; they cannot go on sinning, because they have been born of God.
(1 John 3:9)

Is that hard to take on board? The fact is, despite the guilt we may continue to harbour, our feelings are not always to be trusted – as the Bible reminds us.

The heart is deceitful above all things and beyond cure. Who can understand it?
(Jeremiah 17:9)

I recall the time when, under my father's tuition, I was learning to drive. The road out of town, near where Paul Gallico lived, curved around in a steep bend with stone walls on either side. Again and again, terrified I might hit the wall, I found myself concentrating on it so hard that, inadvertently, I steered towards it.

'Watch the road,' my father urged me, 'not the wall!'

How right he was! By focusing on the thing I feared, I risked a catastrophic collision. Which is what we are in danger of doing if we concentrate on our guilt and sin rather than on the grace and redemption of our Lord Jesus Christ.

Jeff Lucas, author and international speaker, highlights this tendency in us all when, in his Bible notes, *Life Every Day*, he advocates the need to turn our eyes towards God.

This calls for discipline in the way that we use our minds. We can wrongly feel that our minds are in control of us, rather than us being in control of them, taking every thought captive (2 Corinthians 10:5).

*Fear seeks to hijack our self-talk, that inner dialogue that is going on within our minds much of the time. When we talk mentally, we listen to ourselves. Martyn Lloyd Jones once said that '**Most of our unhappiness in life is due to the fact that we listen to ourselves instead of talking to ourselves.**'* (My emphasis.)

Repeating an idea reinforces it in our thinking. And then, because the inner dialogue is coming from us, it comes from a source that we tend to trust: us. We need to monitor and control that internal dialogue, which is admittedly not an easy thing to do, and be willing to give ourselves a good talking to. The psalmist did this, in Psalms 42 and 43, where he asks himself: 'Why, my soul, are you downcast? Why so disturbed within me?' no fewer than three times.

This reminded me of the song I used to sing on the moors in Derbyshire: *Turn your eyes upon Jesus, look full in his wonderful face, and the things of the earth will grow strangely dim, in the light of his glory and grace.*

How I wish I'd put this into practice all those years ago following my divorce. But with the input of the counsellor whose advice I'd sought, I was nearly there. All that remained was for me to take up the prompting of the Holy Spirit, and to move forward in helping those who had shared their loneliness with me in response to my article in the *Church of England Newspaper*. The seeds God had sown in my life were about to be re-sown in that of others. Not only that, they would overflow. For the word I had received from him in my Bible reading was:

Praise be to the God and Father of our Lord Jesus Christ, the Father of compassion and the God of all comfort, who comforts us in all our troubles, so that we can comfort those in any trouble with the comfort we ourselves receive from God. For just as we

share abundantly in the sufferings of Christ, so also our comfort abounds through Christ.
(2 Corinthians 1:3–5)

- How has the kindness of well-meaning friends and family led you into pursuits that were not for you, and have you been able to counter this without falling out?
- What gifts – the seeds sown in your childhood – do you recognise as having put down roots and sent up shoots? In what ways have you been able to nurture them?
- If you know they are there but they still lie dormant, how might you now find a way in which to bring them to fruition?
- Have you ever been hijacked by an inner dialogue of fear and guilt? If so, how have you dealt with it?

GOD'S PURPOSE FOR US?
To convey to others, in word and deed, the Good News of salvation.

23: Fruit Bearing

I am the vine; you are the branches. If you remain in me and I in you, you will bear much fruit; apart from me you can do nothing.
(John 15:5)

In order to fulfil the purpose for which God has picked us, we need to recognise one vital truth. Namely, that it is only in Jesus that we may truly do so. Isca Fellowship, a charismatic church which had begun as a house group and grown to several hundred followers, provided me with the means to remain rooted in Jesus, to branch out and to bear fruit.

Following my letter in the *Church of England Newspaper*, which Stephanie had urged me to write, I'd come across an advertisement giving details of a national fellowship for single Christians. Started by Revd David Lowe, the intention of Christian Friendship and Fellowship was to encourage local groups to set up meetings and activities for anyone who lived alone, be they single, divorced or widowed. Astonished at the way in which I felt this was the Lord affirming my earlier concerns, I talked it through with the minister's wife at Isca and sent off for further details.

Almost immediately, I received a letter from CFF telling me of another member in my vicinity, and suggesting that we meet to discuss the possibility of setting up a local group together. I lost no time in agreeing, and within days Pete was on the phone to me. When a third national member, Christopher, was found to be living nearby, the three of us set up a programme and immediately informed the local churches.

Activities varied enormously, from simple coffee evenings or meals out, to board games and skittles, talks by Traidcraft representatives, or concerts held in local theatres, Exeter University or the cathedral.

Members opened up their homes for the smaller gatherings, and we used church halls for bigger events. Walks on Dartmoor would see large numbers of us meeting together, sharing cars for transport and enjoying a mutual pleasure in God's creation.

For me, one of the main delights was seeing the way in which there was so much fun to be had and so much benefit to all concerned. Within the safe environment of the group, a single father, who rarely saw his children because his ex-wife had moved away, would run around and throw a ball for someone else's children whose father had left them. Another would make them laugh as he acted the clown, leaping across the stepping stones in a stream and generally giving them a hitherto absent male dimension in life.

Equally gratifying was observing the friendship forged between two women who, despite living only a street apart, were unknown to one another previously. One, who had been a carer for her parents for years, had had no chance to socialise while the other, recently widowed, had felt too isolated to venture out.

'My husband died after an eight-year illness,' she said. 'I just couldn't face going out alone, having been shut in for so long. I used to go to bed at eight-thirty every night because I couldn't stand the loneliness. Sleep was a refuge.'

Because they attended different churches, these two women had never come across one another before. The CFF group did, for them and for others, exactly what it was intended to do, bringing Christian friendship and fellowship to their lives.

Gradually, I began to realise that I wanted to take my concern for others further. When I went to a meeting held at church, in which the speaker advocated training for counselling, I knew once again that I had heard the Lord's voice. I signed up there and then, did the training and, ultimately, became a team member of a telephone crisis-intervention counselling service.

Reflections & questions
One of the major changes in my life had come into being as a result

of my attending a Myers Briggs seminar in Exeter. This was at the suggestion of one of Pauline Gates' group when I was still living in my marital home. Aware of my inferiority complex, she felt sure that this might be the answer – and so it was!

Through that simple method, I discovered that my concept of Christianity had always been flawed. To my mind, a born-again believer had to be an extrovert who enthusiastically engaged with large groups and was willingly involved in any number of evangelical activities; a person who thought things through and relied on the practical evidence before them rather than going with a gut-feeling or intuition; someone whose life was structured and well-regulated rather than flexible and spontaneous. How wrong I was!

The fact is that although one body as Christians, we are all unique. Each of us has a different part to play. Some of us may be comparable in the same way as one foot is much like another, or one hand is similar to another. Both perform the same functions, but that does not mean that they are identical. As the Bible reminds us:

There are different kinds of gifts, but the same Spirit distributes them. There are different kinds of service, but the same Lord. There are different kinds of working, but in all of them and in everyone it is the same God at work.
(1 Corinthians 12:5–6)

When we think of the complexity of DNA and read that Abraham offered *his unique son, the one it had been said about, Your seed will be traced through Isaac* (Hebrews 11:17–18 HCSB), we are reminded that each of us is a one-off in God's eyes: precious and distinctive. And when Scripture tells us that the *very hairs of your head are all numbered* (Luke 12:7), and science that blondes have an average of 150,000 (fewer for brunettes and redheads) how can we fail to realise how exclusively we are made?

The guilt I'd felt because I didn't match the Christian criteria I had manufactured was swept away. An INFP myself, I'd long felt inferior in that I found large crowds – such as Sunday worship – quite draining. But put me in a small group, which is the basis from which Isca Fellowship had developed, and I was much more comfortable. Being part of such a group gave me the right environment to absorb and reflect, inwardly, on the behaviour and opinion of others. And from that I was better able to form my own views.

Being an Introvert, I was later to discover, did not necessarily mean you were shy. As I was to learn in years to come, being the speaker at a conference was a completely different concept to being one of a big crowd. For one thing, you were standing alone. For another, you'd been invited to speak. Thus, knowing your audience were expecting to listen, you found the fear of having to chip in had been removed.

Likewise, my iNtuitive manner of conveying and receiving information did not always accord with learning from didactic formulae. No wonder I'd failed at school, because education in those days was a matter of sitting at a desk while being instructed via the blackboard or a text book. My instinctive manner of learning was not by study but by osmosis, visually, verbally and practically. Thus I absorbed what I saw and heard, and assimilated all I put into practice. Imagination played its part. The story of *The Selfish Giant* which my father had read to me as a child, taught me more about selfishness, generosity and the reward of Paradise as I visualised the scenes in my head, than any instruction could ever have done. And just as I'd learned to cook by doing so alongside my mother, so, too, I had learned to speak French fluently when living in France as an au pair.

As a Feeling personality rather than Thinking I was, by *nature*, inclined to go with my instincts when forming judgements or reaching decisions. But in this respect the *nurture* I'd received from my father had allowed me another dimension, in which my intuition forced me to look at both sides of any debate. No wonder, then, that I'd excelled in the debating society at school.

No wonder, either, that my parents – particularly my mother – had found my Perceiving nature so frustrating! While she loved nothing more than a structured life, with a calendar laying out every game of bridge or golf, my 'day-dreaming' tendencies and lack of forward planning infuriated her. An open, flexible, spontaneous approach was my preferred modus operandi but that, too, seemed a misfit with my family. I suppose, since INFPs make up less than four per cent of the British population, it's hardly surprising that I felt so isolated.

Every downside has its up though. Given that INFPs are defined as those who are focused on making the world a better place, with their primary goal that of finding the meaning and purpose of their lives, plus the way in which they might best serve others, it's hardly surprising that this was my ideal when I moved to Exeter. More than anything, I yearned to know what God wanted of me.

- What gifts have you recognised in yourself and used to help others?
- How have your talents, friendships and circumstances come together to reveal God's will for you?
- What rewards have you received in seeing the way your service has benefited others?
- Have you ever taken a personality test to determine your type? How has this helped you to redefine yourself, your skills, and the way in which you perceive others, and the way in which you receive and convey information?

GOD'S PURPOSE FOR US?
To put off the old and put on the new, and thus to know who we are in Christ.

24: Second Cropping

But the fruit of the Spirit is love, joy, peace, forbearance, kindness,
goodness, faithfulness, gentleness and self-control.
(Galatians 5:22–23)

It was clear, right from the start, that Pete and I were destined to be together. One of his comments when he rang me to arrange a meeting for setting up a CFF group was, 'You're not too old to think of remarrying then?' Still in my thirties, I laughed and agreed. But only if the right man were to come along!

Not wishing to take risks with a man I knew nothing about, I arranged to meet him for the first time at a coffee bar in town. I don't recall our conversation but I know we hit it off immediately. A primary school teacher who had recently moved back to his home town, he was easy-going and a good listener. Nevertheless, I was surprised when a man who professed to having been brought up within the strict confines of the Plymouth Brethren, kissed me goodbye when we parted. Even more so, when my heart fluttered and my knees felt weak.

We met on 2nd December less than four months after my move to Exeter. In addition to our CFF meetings, we had numerous outings together and, by Valentine's Day, little more than ten weeks later, Pete was saying, regularly:

'If we got married – not that I'm asking . . .'

It was as if every conversation we had led to the possibility of our union. Unsurprising, I guess, given that we had so much in common. With a shared love of music and nature, a preference for small groups and introverted interaction, and a quiet, reflective stance on the world, we bonded immediately. By 2nd April, exactly four months after meeting, and the day the Falklands War began, the question was popped and we agreed to marry.

Immediately, panic set in. What had I done? Supposing this marriage turned out to be like the last? On the advice of one of my new friends I went for counselling. And with the benefit of talking through the issues in my relationship with James, my fears were settled. Pete took me to choose an engagement ring.

'It had better include rubies,' I laughed, 'because we may be too old to make it to our ruby wedding anniversary.'

In July that year, we married at the local Baptist church and had a fabulous wedding reception put on by my parents in their garden. With Ruth, now fourteen, as my bridesmaid, Sarah's attendance as a guest, and the unexpected arrival of Vicky, my joy was complete.

Throughout Pete's visits to me in Exeter, he and Ruth had forged a relationship which continued after our marriage. Reverting to childhood – she was barely nine when her father left – she would hold Pete's hands and jump on his feet the moment he arrived home from work, insisting he march her around the room. Later, she would make him sit on the floor while she tried to get his foot behind his head as in yoga. Laughter filled our home once more.

Nevertheless, I was fully aware of the place the children's biological father had in their lives. There had been times, when we were still living in the marital home, when James had asked to see the girls and they had complained about the way in which this interfered with their social calendar. For Sarah, whose love of dinghy racing was a regular event, this was particularly the case. But with only Ruth now living at home in Exeter, I encouraged her to see Daddy whenever he asked.

As a tiny tot, she had adored her daddy. With trouser suits the epitome of fashion when she was a little girl, she'd worn them with pride – plus a cut-down tie of Daddy's – and declared that she wanted, one day, to be like him.

Now, however, the comparison between her biological father and stepdad were clearly at odds in her mind. Arriving home from an outing with James, one day, her distress was plain to see.

'What's the matter?' I asked, giving her a hug.

It took a while to coax it out of her, but it transpired that she was full of guilt about her feelings for James and for Pete, fearful that her love for the latter detracted from the former.

'Love isn't finite like a cake,' I explained to her, gently. 'You don't have to cut it into slices and give a piece to everyone. That way, some people might get more than others and some less. Perhaps even none. And one day, you'd run out altogether.'

Then I sang one of the choruses that was popular at the time, 'Love is Something if You Give it away', which says that love is like a magic penny: if you hold on to it you end up with nothing but if you 'spend it' or 'lend it', you'll end up with so much more.

It worked! She got the message. Nevertheless, there were moments when living as a stepfamily was fraught. Pete, used to being greeted with a 'good morning' from his class each day, thought Ruth's silence over breakfast ill-mannered until I explained the differential in time and place. Equally, she had something to learn.

'You don't get to choose what we watch,' she told him one day. 'This is our telly. Mummy's and mine.'

Pete's mother had died when he was in his late teens and his father had remarried. He was, thus, quite savvy about the sort of issues that might be raised in a stepfamily and we had already talked some of them through before our wedding. He had bought a house only a year or so before our marriage and was in the process of doing it up. Given that he was still teaching, and was thus commuting from Exeter each day, common sense might have suggested that we move in with him. There are times, however, when intuitive forethought takes precedence over common sense. It would not work, we decided. Better by far if we put both our homes on the market and started afresh.

Meanwhile, the Gardener was at it again, and a second cropping in our lives was about to nourish others.

Through a couple we met, we started training in Marriage Enrichment, with a view to enhancing our own marriage and, by leading groups, passing on our knowledge to others. This was quite different to Relate or Marriage Guidance in that, although managing conflict constructively was a part of the course, it was not about counselling deteriorating relationships. The emphasis was on the positive: learning how to make the most of what you had and improve upon it.

The topics, some of which are shown here in italics, were varied. One was the fact that *Listening and Hearing* are often not the same thing. They are, though, greatly facilitated by *Feedback*, whereby the listener repeats what they believe the speaker to have been saying. That then gives the speaker the opportunity for confirmation or correction, though we stressed that this should not be undertaken in an aggressive manner.

Likewise, *Knowing and Being Known* require good listening and hearing skills, because there is a degree of vulnerability in sharing one's inner self. Speaking of tenderness, fear, doubt and shame, for example, may not, necessarily, come easily. This is particularly true of men, who are urged to show strength not weakness. But it's true of all of us. Much of this is because these qualities are, by their very nature, intimate not public. They are, therefore, unlikely to have been learned as a component of marriage prior to that union, but are more likely to come about within the intimacy of that relationship.

Which is where *Daily Sharing* comes in, a practice we continue to this day as part of our Quiet Time. Commitment to a *Common Hope* was another aspect of Marriage Enrichment. Likewise, different styles of *Communication* were discussed: shared information; aggressive assertion; feelings.

Some of the issues, when we set up a group, were talked through privately one to one. Others were up for debate within the group. We devised quiz sheets for partnership potential, whereby couples ringed the words that best described how they saw themselves. And then their spouse. In addition to couple-related activities, individual pursuits were explored as a means of enriching a relationship.

'If you're joined at the hip and do everything together, you've nothing new to bring into your marriage,' we explained.

The importance of tactile and vocal expressions of love was paramount. Still, to this day (thirty-six years after our marriage), Pete and I indulge in what we humorously call 'kitchen cuddles and kisses' and 'hugs in the hall'.

Less than two years after my move to Exeter, and only nine months after Pete and I had married, we decided to move. By the time our houses had sold, we'd pooled resources and bought a four-bedroomed detached house, we'd set up a Marriage Enrichment course and a Christian singles group. What's more, despite telling our singles that this was *not* a dating agency, we'd seen no fewer than eight happy marriages emerge from those events. Ours included. But was that happiness to last? That was the question.

Reflections & questions

Looking back, it never ceases to amaze us that, having known one another for only seven-and-a-half months prior to our union, we have now celebrated what we agree is thirty-six years of the happiest and most fulfilling period of our lives. How much of that was down to our Marriage Enrichment training, I don't know. But it is an exercise I would encourage all married couples to undertake.

Statistics in 2014 showed stepfamilies to be in the decline, with a rise in cohabiting. The result is that almost 4.2 million children do not live with both parents. Family life is increasingly complicated these days and while blended families can be very fulfilling, they require greater understanding than biological relationships.

One of the books I wrote years later, titled *Stepfamilies* and published by Lion, looks at many of the issues raised by the families who have faced them and, as a result, I have been asked quite often to take part in radio panel shows and phone-ins. My advice, always, has been to encourage anyone undertaking a second marriage to put as much thought as possible into their relationship and their future stepfamily before signing on the dotted line. Now, with fewer people going down the route of binding relationships, that advice still stands. Think through the issues that are likely to arise. List them. Talk to one another. Adult to adult. Adult to child. Learn from one another. If possible, see a counsellor. Or read the many blogs I've written on the subject.

And remember the scripture at the start of this chapter:

But the fruit of the Spirit is love, joy, peace, forbearance, kindness, goodness, faithfulness, gentleness and self-control.
(Galatians 5:22–23)

- Have you ever made a decision as momentous as Pete's and my marriage in so short a time, believing it to be the result of the Lord's guiding hand? How did it turn out?
- What do you know about listening and hearing; knowing and being known?
- Is this something you put into practice in your marriage? Indeed, in all your relationships?
- Could a regular Quiet Time, with Bible notes, discussion, prayer time and sharing be of help in this respect?
- Are you part of a stepfamily, or do you know of stepfamilies who have made a success of their relationships? What do you put this down to?

GOD'S PURPOSE FOR US?
To grant us the benefit of his loving nature so that we, by his Holy Spirit, might become like him.

Feed My Sheep
1983–88

25: Offshoots

He cuts off every branch in me that bears no fruit, while every branch that does bear fruit he prunes so that it will be even more fruitful.
(John 15:2)

It was a telephone call in the middle of the night, not long after Pete, Ruth and I had moved, that alerted me to the severity of Vicky's problems. A miniature 'life and soul of the party' as was her father, she was an absolute delight as a toddler but had never been the easiest of children to raise. Always one to put you to the test, she would take every instruction as a challenge. So when told not to touch an electric plug, or to speak to a stranger, she would do just that, taking great delight in proving you wrong.

'I touched a plug and I not 'lectocuted,' she would say, triumphantly. Or,

'I talked to that man, and he no take me away.'

Taking it too far on one occasion, when she'd climbed to the top shelf of the cupboard in which I kept medicines, she'd ended up in hospital having her stomach pumped!

James, who had adored Sarah when she was born, had later turned his back on her in favour of Vicky. 'Goody-two-shoes' was one of the names he'd applied to Sarah, and it was a refrain taken up later by Vicky when she accused me of favouring her sister. The fact was that, try as I might throughout her childhood, I simply couldn't fathom Vicky. We had little in common to bond us, whereas Sarah and I shared a love of reading and an introvert personality and Ruth was my adorable little clown.

Nevertheless, when James' and Sarah's shared love of sailing in the estuary meant that Vicky was dropped by her father, my concern had been for her. Particularly when Vicky's ineptitude with anchors and guy ropes had earned her the nickname You-Fool from her father. Perhaps, like my father, I always had an eye for the underdog. The more so when it had come to Vicky's schooling at the convent. While Sarah had showed great promise academically, Vicky larked about and achieved little. Except when it came to propping a packet of flour on top of the door and waiting for one of the nun's to come in. Or, of course, her art!

'I just wonder if Vicky is viewed unfavourably,' I'd said to James when I was still living in our old home and he'd remarried. 'They're bound to make comparisons with Sarah.'

We'd talked about the possibility of Vicky attending a local College of Arts where her considerable skill in drawing and painting might have come to the fore. The only problem was that it had a reputation for drugs and immorality, and in the end nothing had come of our discussion.

Sarah, meanwhile, had achieved excellent marks for her O-levels but the sixth form at the boarding school she and Vicky attended did not have good results. So her only choice was to go to the local grammar school in order to take her A-levels. My meeting with the head of the sixth form had not gone well! I'd had no option but to turn again to James.

'She made it pretty clear that she had no time for privately educated pupils,' I told him. 'Perhaps she'll take more notice of you.'

She had! But she hadn't made it easy for Sarah.

Nevertheless, Sarah had done well for herself, passed her A-levels and, prior to my marriage to Pete, had been living and working in London. Now, with our move away from Exeter, she asked if she could come back home. So, there we were, newly married with a stepfamily.

At Vicky's request, when she left school, I'd pleaded to have her accepted on a hairdressing course at the technical college in Plymouth but, within months, she'd thrown in the towel. Choosing, instead, to live in squalor in a shared squat, she was jobless and virtually penniless. But despite everything, I'd managed to stay in touch with her.

'What sort of family life have I ever had with you and dad rowing all the time,' she yelled when I visited her.

Tears welled in my eyes, but my apologies rang hollow in her ears and she recoiled from any attempt on my part to reach out to her physically.

'If you do nothing and Vicky wrecks her life, she'll always hold you responsible,' my parents had told me when Vicky first started going astray.

Since she was still a minor, I had to agree. But then there were Christian friends who urged me to leave her be and put my trust in the Lord.

I'd done my best to convey my love and care for my daughter but nothing, it seemed, could shake off the moniker by which I'd been labelled by the psychiatrist: that of a religiously over-zealous mother. Equally absurd was the law. Following Vicky's arrest for brawling and her involvement with the leader of a gang of bikers who had been accused of taking part in the gang-rape of a girl on the beach, I'd sought the help of social services. Pointing out that she was only sixteen and was without a job or an income, I'd found their response incomprehensible. Despite the law stating that a minor could not leave home unless they could support themselves, it appeared that it was perfectly acceptable for the Welfare State to provide that financial support at the taxpayers' expense.

'So you're telling me that the tax I pay may be used to help my daughter run away from home?' I said. 'You do know she's involved with a man who's awaiting trial for rape?'

'I'm very sorry,' the social worker responded. 'At sixteen she's considered out of moral danger. She can see whoever she wants.'

Words failed me! But it didn't end there. So when sometime later she was in trouble again, it was hardly a surprise.

Following Vicky's indictment in respect of the theft of prescription drugs from a local surgery, her father and I were asked to consider making her a ward of court. The idea, put to us by the solicitor acting on her behalf, was to spare her a spell in prison. Apparently, she had 'only' acted as look-out for the gang, hence the leniency of a suspended sentence, but this, we were told, would necessitate one of us having Vicky to live with us. I knew if Pete and I were to agree to give her a home that it would be unfair on Ruth who was still at school. Equally, from the gossip doing the rounds, I somewhat doubted that James' parenting (or marriage) skills had improved.

I'd never denied James parental rights to see his children. Indeed, at times, I'd had to push the girls into seeing him when his wishes had encroached upon theirs. At the same time, I worried. He and his wife continued to be heavy drinkers and it was not a habit I wanted to encourage in my children. Nor to embrace the 'open marriage' lifestyle that Sheila boasted they now practised.

As it happened, my concern was well-founded. It appeared that initially the courts had liaised with Sheila, believing her to be Vicky's mother. Plus, I had good reason to suspect that James had already cut a deal in which he was to have Vicky living with him. Consequently, I had little option but to agree.

Within months the probation order had been broken and Vicky had run away. Inevitably, the story that emerged had two sides. Meeting with me, she told me that her father had made a violent, drunken assault on her and she had vowed never to return. Seeing the wounds that had been inflicted, I could only respond with love.

But when James rang me a day or two later, I learned that the fight between them had started because he had been steaming open Vicky's post from the imprisoned rapist.

'We had a blazing row,' he said. 'Even I was shocked with the contents. She's been visiting him in prison. I told her I was going to lock her in her room.'

It seems it had all escalated from there. Vicky had left her father's home, and had been living in London for some time.

* * *

Now aged twenty, and with the young man still in prison, Vicky had continued to live a profligate lifestyle in London. Thus her phone call, in the middle of the night, set my heart hammering as I sat up and put the receiver to my ear.

'It's me – Vicky,' came the voice down the line. 'Mum, I can't come home for Christmas.'

A first for Pete, we were due to spend Christmas with my parents as usual.

'Is it the train fare, darling?' I asked, intending to offer to pay it.

'No, Mum. I'm so sorry. I don't know how to tell you.'

She broke down and wept. My heart raced.

'What is it, darling?'

'I'm on heroin, Mum,' her tears stopped; her voice hardened. 'I'm mainlining. Injecting regularly.'

The darkness of the room closed in on me. I'd known for some time that she had experimented with cannabis, but had no idea it had gone this far. Struggling with a rising sense of nausea, I learned that she'd been using heroin for two years.

'I want to stop,' she continued. 'Mum, I'm so frightened. Will you help?'

Given the acrimony that had existed between us since her father's departure, and the way in which all the blame had been laid at my door, I could hardly believe that she was now turning to me for help. Begging me not to tell my parents, she promised only to take oral substances and not to inject while staying with them over Christmas.

'I can't do that, Vicky,' I said. 'I can't take you undercover into their home, with all your cousins staying too. They have a right to know.'

Somehow, with Pete's and my parents support, we got through the festival as a family. And when Vicky asked me to speak to our doctor about methadone, I willingly did so. If only that had been the end of it.

Reflections & questions

The trauma of seeing your child – the child you've brought into the world, nurtured, loved and cared for – squander all life has to offer is immense. Vicky's lifestyle, over the years, had also taken its toll on Ruth. Despite her persistent attempt to hide her feelings to spare me, her distress was obvious. Now, with Vicky's revelation that she was a heroin addict, the question was, what to do? Turning to what the Bible had to say, I read:

There was a man who had two sons. The younger one said to his father, 'Father, give me my share of the estate.' So he divided his property between them. Not long after that, the younger son got together all he had, set off for a distant country and there squandered his wealth in wild living.
(Luke 15:11–13)

For years, there were those who had told me I had to keep trying to get Vicky to come home; others who spoke of letting her go and trusting her to the Lord. Yet it seemed to me, in the parable of the Prodigal Son, that the father not only released his younger son to live his own life, he actually provided him with the means to do so. Which, of course, is what God does for us.

I'd tried both responses with my daughter, and was to continue doing so for many years to come. On every occasion that she turned to us for help, we were there to give it. Just as the father had done when his younger son realised his error and returned home.

So he got up and went to his father. But while he was still a long way off, his father saw him and was filled with compassion for him; he ran to his son, threw his arms around him and kissed him.
(Luke 15:20)

The fact was, the father had never stopped loving his son. Just as God had never abandoned me when I fell from grace. So how could I do so with my daughter?

- Is this freedom and support to 'do your own thing' something you have ever experienced in your life? Is it something you have granted to your offspring?
- Did it work out well for you/them? Or did you/they, like the prodigal son, live to regret it?
- If so, did you/they seek forgiveness and find the way home?

GOD'S PURPOSE FOR US?
Never to give up on those we love.

26: Grain And Grapes Make Bread And Wine

This is to my Father's glory, that you bear much fruit, showing yourselves to be my disciples.
(John 15:8)

Despite the difficulties with Vicky I had never stopped writing and, following my marriage to Pete and our move from Exeter, I'd had a word from the Lord: *See to it that you finish the good work.* I took this to be in respect of the book I had been putting together with the help of Derek, from Inter Varsity Press. It seemed that in the Gardener's hands, the fruit I bore for him was now about to be shared with others. On hearing my story during the time Pete and I had been courting, John, a friend of his parents and a well-known speaker and evangelist, encouraged me to seek publication. His enthusiasm, as he read through my typed manuscript, was hard to resist. With some fear and trepidation, I put forward my work and was astonished when, with certain provisos, it was accepted.

The book, I was told, was to be split into two: one giving the story of my marriage; the other that of my divorce. Prayerfully I considered the idea, aware as I did so, that in writing *my* story, I would be revealing secrets and uncovering hitherto hidden circumstances that belonged to *others*. At the same time, I knew that if I was to bear fruit for the farmer whose scattered seed had thrived, and be a branch of the vine which had given me life, I had to throw off the British stiff upper lip and the middle-class concept of discretion with which I was raised, and embrace the vulnerability demanded of me by the Gardener.

My prayers were answered. Realising that the use of a pseudonym would go some way to protect my identity, while a change of name for each person in the story would protect those of my family, I signed not one, but two contracts and set about the required re-write. In due course, they were published. The first told the story of the tensions involved in being unequally yoked in marriage; the second the way in which the Lord had undertaken for me and the girls on the break-up of our family – despite the Christian ethos in respect of divorce.

Once again, via my publisher, I received a barrage of mail: letters from all over the world, telling me how grateful my readers were to learn of the way in which I had not only survived but thrived; sharing stories of their plight. Always, I replied in kind. Since my baptism in the Holy Spirit, I had learned to listen to the Lord; to hear his voice; to obey his commands. The reward of seeing results, knowing that I was helping others, was a thrill beyond measure.

I wish I could say the same for the attention this brought me. An author, in the days pre-internet and self-publishing, was considered a celebrity. People at the large Baptist church we now attended, clamoured to speak to me, enthralled with the aura of fame and acclaim in which they saw me. Inwardly and outwardly I shrank. Embarrassed and awkward, I refuted what I saw as their misperception. Our minister, Revd David Coffey, would have none of it. Prayerfully involved in the ongoing situation with Vicky, he encouraged me to write her story.

'But it has no ending,' I argued, 'happy or otherwise.'

'It's a journey,' David told me. 'A journey travelled with God. It doesn't need an ending. It will encourage others to put their trust in the Lord while they're still on the way.'

Again, I relied on the Lord for a title, aware, as I did so, that it was this that had furnished me with the theme of each book. So while *The Tug of Two Loves* had spoken of the tug-of-war in loving God and an unbeliever, and *Divorced But Not Defeated* conveyed the way in which the anathema between discipleship and divorce was a foe to be overcome, *Where is My Child?* published by Kingsway, was to do just what David had suggested. The idea of a journey with

God and the uncertainty of the destination was expressed in the nature of the question, just as the idea of travelling together was communicated throughout the narrative.

Again, the book was incredibly well-received. Utilising my own experience, I began to write articles for magazines on debt, divorce and drugs. And having trained in counselling, I now became part of a team which met weekly in an open-door policy in the church lounge, helping anyone who turned up to cope with the problems they faced.

Another book followed, *Second Marriage* published by Kingsway, in which I shared the issues Pete and I had faced over the years we'd been married, plus those of four other couples who had remarried. Using the analogy of building a house, I wrote of the necessity of *Viewing the Site* and *Preparing the Ground* – the inner healing that's required when an earlier marriage has broken down. Then came a chapter on *Family Foundations* – a sensitive approach to breaking the news of remarriage to the family; *Establishing an Equitable Economy* – budgeting, maintenance, wills, and so on and so forth. Coping with conflict and letting go of guilt; manipulative behaviour; access with absent parents and the split loyalties this entails; the legalities; grandparents – the old and the new; all are factors that have to be faced.

With a Foreword written by Canon Max Wigley, which began: *This book is long overdue . . . The author has successfully and realistically tackled the problems faced by people who remarry following either divorce or the death of their first partner,* the book met with great acclaim. Revd Nick Mercer, Director of Training at London Bible College, described it as a *splendid little book* and, in a letter to me, wrote:

Were I still Review Editor of Today Magazine, *I would review it, but alas, I am not. But I will certainly add it to our Pastoral Theology reading and reference list.*

One of the issues raised in the book was what happens when the daughter of a broken home is planning her wedding. This was a subject we'd had to address when Sarah announced that she was to be married.

'I know I always said I wouldn't want Dad to give me away . . .' she began, her agitation evident in the way she twisted the engagement ring on her finger.

Now, despite all that had gone before, it became clear that Sarah's father, rather than stepfather, should be the one to give his daughter away. And so it was that on a sunny summer's day, I watched my eldest set off for church in a horse-drawn carriage from Cockington, a medieval village in the valley, to be launched into a new life.

Little did I know how this was to impact on both Sarah and Vicky. Yet again, the Gardener had scattered seeds, some on rocky paths, others that were to survive and thrive.

Reflections & questions

Friends told me that writing my testimony would be cathartic. And so it was! But the fact is that writing was not an activity to me; it *was* me! My introvert nature; my love of books; my personal experience of the power of story, endorsed by author, Dorothea Brande – and by Jesus, himself – combined to make a compelling force in my life. Add to that the command I'd received from the Lord, 'to comfort others with the comfort I'd received', and how could I help but believe that this was the purpose for which I'd been picked? To share with others the sinfulness and sufferings of my life, and the way in which the Father had forgiven, comforted and led me. In this way, the fruit I bore as a disciple when writing books and articles, was to nourish others and thus show the Father's glory (John 15:8).

But that is not to say that this is the only fruit to be found; nor the only way in which it may be used. Apples are for crunching into as they are; for peeling and cooking as in apple crumble; for fermenting and making into cider to drink. Likewise grapes may be eaten fresh, dried as raisins, or made into wine. Wheat, too, may become flour which, in turn, might become bread, cereal, cake or biscuits. There's no end of variety and usage.

As we saw in Chapter 22, the fruit of the Spirit is equally diverse, being described in Galatians 5:22–23 as *love, joy, peace, forbearance, kindness, goodness, faithfulness, gentleness and self-control*. That theme is taken up, also, in 1 Corinthians 12:1

> *Now about the gifts of the Spirit, brothers and sisters, I do not want you to be uninformed* and again in 12:4–6 *There are different kinds of gifts, but the same Spirit distributes them. There are different kinds of service, but the same Lord. There are different kinds of working, but in all of them and in everyone it is the same God at work.*

All, we are told, are the work of the same Spirit, but they are distributed to each one as he sees fit.

It's interesting that the later verses distinguish between gifts, service and working. In helping others, through my books or via counselling, I was fulfilling the work God had given me to do. But so, too, were other occurrences in my life. Such as standing on the platform in the Underground with a child who had become separated from his mother who was aboard the train and was trying, frantically, to open the locked doors. 'I'll wait with him until you return,' I mouthed through the glass window as the train set off. Or buying a pasty for someone on the street who is obviously in need. Or simply smiling and exchanging a few words to passers-by. All come under the umbrella of discipleship and fruitfulness.

Others are harder. Which was why we decided to give James a second chance at Sarah's wedding. It wasn't easy seeing the man who had deserted us walking down the aisle with my daughter on his arm; nor having the woman who had destroyed my marriage and her husband's life, seated at the top table at the reception. But showing forbearance, kindness and self-control was every bit as fruitful, and brought as much glory to God I'm sure, as was being an author. And it was to pay off! In more ways than one.

- The gifts of the Spirit are what God has given us, the service the way in which he inspires us to use them. What are your gifts? How are you using them in service for others in order to bring glory to God?
- How does the analogy of apples, grapes and grain and the diverse ways in which each may be used help you to understand your fruitfulness better?
- Have you ever had to show the fruits of the Spirit in an encounter with an unbeliever who has caused chaos and distress in your life?

GOD'S PURPOSE FOR US?
Always to be open to new ways of service when it comes to using our gifts.

27: A Clear Path

*Trust in the LORD with all your heart and lean not on your own
understanding; in all your ways submit to him, and he will make
your paths straight.*
(Proverbs 3:5–6)

Much had happened with Vicky during the six or seven years since
Pete and I had married. On one occasion, en route to Gatwick
Airport, Ruth and I visited her in a slum area of London, and there
was no escaping just how far she had sunk. At Vicky's request, I
had agreed that we would stay overnight in the flat she shared with
another young woman, but the squalor was such that I advised Ruth
to spread a towel over the pillow and to keep her dressing gown
on. My fears were well-founded. With sadness in her voice, Vicky's
flatmate assured me that my daughter had not had to sink so low
as to sell her body. Which, I took it, was exactly what this girl was
doing.

On another occasion, Vicky disappeared altogether. For weeks
we completely lost touch with her. Frantic phone calls to known
contacts revealed nothing as to her whereabouts, and even the
Salvation Army's missing persons team were unable to provide any
leads. It wasn't the first time. And it wasn't the last. On yet another
occasion, following a phone call informing me that Vicky had been
admitted to University College Hospital and wasn't expected to last
the night, James and I set off together believing this would be the
end. It wasn't!

Three times Vicky had begged for help to get her off drugs, and
three times Pete and I had taken her in, loved her, cared for her,

endeavoured to help her with her methadone and rehabilitation programme. More than once, she had gone out alone during the day and failed to come home in the evening. Anxiously, we would be scouring the town, terrified that we'd find her dead in a doorway.

She'd also had a spell in a mental hospital. Intended by the doctors who sent her there to be an aid in ending her addiction, it was a truly terrifying experience. I visited her daily, saw the patients around her who lay thrashing about on the floor, while the air screeched with the cries of those who, for their own safety and that of the other inhabitants and staff, were locked in their rooms. Visiting Brunel's Atmospheric Railway in Dawlish, I'd take Vicky out for tea – anything to get her away. Then came the day of my father's birthday.

'I must visit him,' I said, 'so I won't be in to see you that day.'

Disaster! Unbeknown to me, Vicky contacted a male friend, arranged his visit with the nursing staff, and succeeded in leaving the premises. She never returned.

Some years earlier, following an appeal from the front at our Baptist church, Sarah had gone forward for baptism by immersion. It was a real answer to prayer. Though I'd led a far from sinless life myself, I'd never reneged on my promise to God when she had encephalitis that I would bring her up to know and love him. As with all my children. So it was a great thrill to see her journey of faith. She'd been to Spring Harvest, attended All Souls Church when living in London, and now felt ready to affirm her commitment.

But what of my other children, I thought? And then, as Sarah was about to go beneath the waters of baptism, I'd had a vision. It was of a beach at the seaside, gentle waves lapping upon the shore. All three of my girls paddling at the edge. And then I saw a net and above it a giant hand. One by one, each of my beloved daughters was raised, placed in the net, and lifted on high.

Interpretation of the vision was instantaneous. The paddling represented the prayerful tuition I had given them throughout their childhood; the hand was the hand of God; the net was his assurance of their safety with him. And so he was to prove.

Within a year of her marriage, we learned that Sarah was expecting her first child. Due in October, this meant that she would be at the end of her first trimester, about to go into the second, during the lambing season.

'I mustn't go anywhere near the ewes while they're pregnant,' she told me. 'There's a high risk that I could contract toxoplasmosis and miscarry. That means I can't help with lambing.'

Not being versed in farming procedures, I knew nothing of this. But when Sarah asked Vicky if she would help with lambing, I instantly recognised God's hand.

Vicky, as a child, had loved animals.

'I going to be a vet when I grow up,' she would say, full of enthusiasm.

So when farming friends offered to take her on during the lambing season, she'd jumped at the chance. And every spring until James left, she'd helped out on the rolling Devon hills alongside the estuary.

Learning of Sarah's predicament, Vicky lost no time in coming home to us in preparation for her visit to the farm in Wales. She looked gaunt and grey, her little moon-face – my nickname for her as a child – now thin and shrunken. Her arms bore evidence of needles. Her eyes were dead.

Once again, I had a message from the Lord, not visually this time but as a voice inside. Sitting on the end of our bed, I shared it with Pete.

'I believe the Lord is telling me that we have to let go of Vicky. That we must explain that she's on her own. We can't give her any more help,' I said.

Pete sat beside me and took my hand in his.

'Are you sure about this?' His face looked drawn.

I explained that I felt God was telling me that we had to re-think how we dealt with Vicky; that he was the Rock; and that in constantly giving her help and support, we were behaving like a cushion that prevented her from reaching Rock-bottom.

'Jesus is the Rock. And it's only going to happen if she gets to Rock-bottom and takes responsibility for herself,' I finished.

We prayed together and, to my surprise, Pete broke down and wept with me.

I shared this word from the Lord with one of our church elders.

'It's the hardest thing I've ever been asked to do,' I said. 'Please pray for us.'

The evening before Vicky was due to depart for Wales, she went out on a binge in town. On her return, I sat her down, held her hands in mine, and told her what I'd told Pete.

'We love you,' I began. 'And we always will. But we can't keep helping you like this. You have to do it yourself, darling.'

Wrenching her hands away, she stood over me and bawled, pouring out all the hatred and vitriol of the past years. Then she left home for the bus-station and her midnight departure for Wales.

Months later when lambing was over, Vicky returned, briefly, to London.

'There were no drugs in Wales,' she told me, recounting the story. 'Nothing! So I've been clean all this time. I had no choice. When I went back to see my friends, it was as if my eyes were opened. I saw them for the first time as they really were. They were zombies. All of them.'

She returned to Wales and enrolled herself in agricultural college with a view to working towards fulfilling her childhood love of animals. Two years later, I went to her graduation. And though she never did take up farm work, earning her living in other ways, to God's glory she remained drug free and independent.

Reflections & Questions

Throughout Vicky's years of drug abuse, I was convinced that the loving thing to do was to help her come clean. I still, to this day, believe that it was right. Had we left her to her own devices at that stage of the game, who knows what would have happened? She would, almost certainly, have felt unloved and rejected. Worthless of anything other than the chaotic life she lived.

It was only once she was assured of our love that the time came for us to let go and let God. The problem, the Lord revealed to me, was that every time we helped Vicky to detox from her heroin addiction, it was like the man who swept his house clean.

> *When an impure spirit comes out of a person, it goes through arid places seeking rest and does not find it. Then it says, 'I will return to the house I left.' When it arrives, it finds the house unoccupied, swept clean and put in order. Then it goes and takes with it seven other spirits more wicked than itself, and they go in and live there. And the final condition of that person is worse than the first.*
> (Matthew 12:43–45)

Sweeping her clean of drugs three times, as we had, was not the entire answer. Being left devoid of the highs she had known while on drugs, it was only natural that she should seek the presence of those she believed to be her friends. People of like mind. People still on drugs. And what more natural than that they should fill her with what she lacked? More heroin.

It was only when, swept clean of drugs because none were available in Wales, that the void was filled in other ways. Ways that were meaningful and fulfilling to her. Living with family. Helping on the farm. Having positive input from her sister, Sarah. And later going through college.

I recently asked the Book Club I lead to read a book titled *When Helping Hurts* by Steve Corbett and Brian Fikkert. Without exception, we found the ethos incredibly illuminating. Highlighting the need to identify the principles of poverty alleviation, the authors brought to our attention the damage that can be done by responding in the wrong way. Crisis intervention and 'fixing the problem' is not always appropriate, while rehabilitation or development are seen to be more successful. As is identifying the assets of those in need – the gifts that they might bring to the situation – so that in doing so they might, ultimately, know they have value and wholeness.

In the end, it was this that worked for Vicky. It was a painful lesson for us all to learn, but one that brought about a happy conclusion. At least for some years.

- Addictions vary: drugs, alcohol, sugar, pornography, etc. How would you have advocated dealing with this prior to reading about my experience?
- If coming off an addiction cold-turkey is not the solution if there is nothing positive to replace it, what assets (gifts) could you identify in someone in need?
- Do you believe that there are times when even an addict can have their eyes opened to reality – as Paul did on the road to Damascus, and as Vicky did on her return to London. How could you help to confront someone you know with that reality?

GOD'S PURPOSE FOR US?
At the right time, to trust God enough to stop being the cushion, and allow our loved ones to reach Rock-bottom in the belief that he is the Rock.

Sunset & Evening Star

1989–1994

28: A Plum Job

When you come together, each one has a hymn, a lesson, a revelation, a tongue, or an interpretation. Let all things be done for building up.
(1 Corinthians 14:26 ESV)

A year or so after Vicky's miraculous recovery, I received a letter from Hodder & Stoughton. Having heard of my previous books, James Catford, Commissioning Editor, asked if I would ghost-write the testimony of a young woman living in my vicinity. Her name was Susan James and she was resident in a Cheshire Home in Brixham, Torbay.

The Bay, in South Devon, is approximately five miles across, is well sheltered from the prevailing winds and thus has a wonderful history. Evidence in Kent's Cavern shows that it was inhabited in Palaeolithic times 40,000 years ago; the Romans landed here when Britain was part of the Roman Empire; it appears in the Domesday Book; Torre Abbey, a monastery built in the 12th century, still stands; and William of Orange, whose statue stands on the quay in Brixham, landed on its southern coast in 1688, during the Glorious Revolution, when he declared that: *The Liberties of England and The Protestant Religion I Will Maintain*. It also saw the embarkation of Napoleon when he was exiled to St Helena. Known as The English Riviera, it is a stunningly beautiful and much loved tourist resort.

I duly visited Susan at Douglas House and learned of her story. A local girl, her older sister was one of the twenty-one Sunday school children killed during World War II, when German planes off-loaded bombs on St Marychurch, Torquay. Decades later, Susan married a young man from nearby and the two of them moved to Ecuador where they lived a life of luxury. Sadly, over time, their relationship deteriorated and ended in divorce. Susan returned to the UK, where she began to experience dizzy turns. Surgery to remove the tumour that was found to be growing in her brain rendered her paralysed.

Not yet thirty, embittered, and wondering what point there was in her life, Susan was wheelchair bound: a paraplegic. Ten years later her father died and her mother went into a residential care home. Then Susan met a man in her own care home who was bed-bound. He told her about Jesus and, in due course, Susan became a believer and was baptised. She began to write poetry and became a speaker, sharing her testimony. Eventually, she met with Joni Eareckson Tada, a woman whose paralysis, as the result of a diving accident, had made her a celebrity.

It was a moving story and one I felt I could write with the passion and sincerity it deserved. What's more, I had met one of Hodder's authors at a writers' conference, and he agreed to read and comment on the manuscript. Thus, Hugh Rae, who wrote novels under the pen-name Jessica Stirling, became a firm friend and we corresponded for years to come. Meanwhile, Susan's book, titled *Healed Within*, was published and, as a result, she and I appeared together on BBC *Songs of Praise*, and we were later approached by another TV company wanting to film her story.

It was agreed that I was to interview her. And as we met with the producer and cameraman on Berry Head, the most southerly point of Torbay, Susan was reminded of a vision she had had there years earlier. It was of an angel – a man, dressed in a suit on a hot summer's day – who had told her that Jesus loved her.

'I didn't want to know,' Susan said, 'but God refused to take no for an answer. He sought me out. He made me his own. He saved me, primarily to be his child, to know him and love him.'

'But,' she finished, 'I was also to be his hands. His feet. His love. I was to be part of a greater whole. My focus was not to be taken up with the work God required of me, but with the Lord himself.'

Despite her disablement, Susan had been picked for a purpose. And she knew it!

A year or so later, James Catford asked me write another book. It was the story of a young scientist, a haemophiliac who, while working in the USA as a post-graduate from Oxford, became HIV+ as a result of contaminated bloods. Taking up a post with Glaxo, in Geneva, he subsequently developed AIDS and died, leaving a wife and young daughter. But neither he, nor his wife, ever lost faith in the Lord.

I declined. It was too distressing. James begged me to read the journals Phil and Jana Godfrey had kept. He was convinced I could do the story justice. Eventually I agreed and when the documents arrived through the post early one Saturday morning, I sat in bed in tears as I read it through. I knew without a shadow of doubt that I had to do it.

Hodder asked me to go to Geneva, at their expense, where Phil's widow, Jana, still lived.

'My daddy's with the Lord Jesus,' said his little daughter when they met me at the airport. 'And he's got new legs.'

Living with Jana and visiting the World Health Organisation, Glaxo, and other important places in Phil's life, I did my research and pieced together the sequence of events. Later I went to stay with his family in Oxford. It was harrowing, but at the same time uplifting. I learned that Phil, and two other scientists working at Glaxo, were responsible for discovering dopamine receptors, crucial knowledge in devising the treatment of Parkinson's and similar diseases.

One of the reviews, written by an American when the book was finally published, described it as: *so moving and so well written; conveys all the agony and trials of AIDS so well and the everyday details of coping and caring; the mental, emotional and spiritual struggles are all followed and interwoven so as to give an effective, vibrant, multi-coloured picture of actual events. A literal can't put down book.*

In due course, it became a *Sunday Times* No. 4 bestseller but, perhaps more importantly, it eventually helped in some way to change the social stigma and unjust anomalies associated with HIV and AIDS. While visiting Parliament as the guest of my local MP, Rupert Allason (also an author) to undertake research for another book I was writing, I learned that mortgages, life assurance and so forth were hugely restricted for the families of AIDS sufferers, and that this was something John Major was determined to change when he came into power.

The fame that this book afforded me was enormous but, as before, I shrank when in the limelight. Edward England, one of the most influential Christian publishers at the time, introduced me at a large conference as a 'bestselling author'. I cringed.

'I'm not,' I spluttered. 'The book was a bestseller. Not me.'

My interpretation was firmly refuted by Edward; and later, David Coffey, my church pastor and friend, told me off.

'Don't hide your light under a bushel,' he said. 'It's not yours to hide.'

This, I later learned, was a reference to one of Jesus' parables, in which he told his listeners:

Neither do people light a lamp and put it under a bowl. Instead they put it on its stand, and it gives light to everyone in the house. (Matthew 5:15)

Reflections & questions

What David Coffey had to say to me was, perhaps, one of the most important things I was to learn. In conjunction with the instruction the Lord had given me 'to comfort others with the comfort I had received', he set me on a path to do just that. Being a shrinking violet and hiding what God has done for us and through us is not on. How else would we ever have learned of Christ and salvation had we not had the stories of the Bible recorded for us? It's not *our* glory we proclaim when we tell of God's work in our lives. It is *his*!

In the belief that this is a vital truth in being picked for a purpose, and with a strong desire to reach out to non-believers, I started writing crossover novels. The first, titled *Time to Shine*, focuses on this theme. This was in response to a word I had from the Lord, in which he told me to *entertain your readers so they will absorb truths they might otherwise resist.* The book became a No. 1 Bestseller in its category on Amazon, and the Word I had received was later confirmed when I was interviewed on Premier Radio, and Christy Wimber was quoted as saying: 'Truths are better caught than taught.'

My hope was that my readers would catch on to the fact that we are all meant to shine. With permission from the author, Marianne Williamson, I have included the following quotation in the story:

Our deepest fear is not that we are inadequate. Our deepest fear is that we are powerful beyond measure. It is our light, not our darkness that most frightens us. We ask ourselves, 'Who am I to be brilliant, gorgeous, talented, fabulous?' Actually, who are you not to be? You are a child of God. Your playing small does not serve the world. There is nothing enlightened about shrinking so that other people won't feel insecure around you. We are all meant to shine, as children do. We were born to make manifest the glory of God that is within us. It's not just in some of us; it's in everyone. And as we let our own light shine, we unconsciously give other people permission to do the same. As we are liberated from our own fear, our presence automatically liberates others.

The seed that God scattered in Susan James' life, with the vision of an angel on Berry Head, fell on stony ground and was pecked away by the crows. But God didn't give up! Despite her refusal to listen, he went on to sow more seed through the man in her care home. And despite the physical weaknesses imposed upon her by her brain tumour, he chose *her* to shame the things which are strong.

Brothers and sisters, think of what you were when you were called. Not many of you were wise by human standards; not many were influential; not many were of noble birth. But God chose the foolish things of the world to shame the wise; God

chose the weak things of the world to shame the strong. God chose the lowly things of this world and the despised things – and the things that are not – to nullify the things that are, so that no one may boast before him. It is because of him that you are in Christ Jesus, who has become for us wisdom from God – that is, our righteousness, holiness and redemption. Therefore, as it is written: 'Let the one who boasts boast in the Lord.'
(1 Corinthians 1:26–31)

Like Susan James, we all have to learn that it is not what we *do* that is important to God. Neither is it what we know. It's who we are! Who we are *in him*! But it follows that if we are to be the people God wants us to be, we must not shrink from the work he puts before us. And neither should we shrink from glorifying God. As I write this, Prince Harry has just shared his mental health issues in respect of his mother's death: a brave admission which, rightly, brought him much praise and respect.

Whilst having coffee with friends in one of the seafront hotels last year, I noticed a woman sitting alone. It worried me! Before leaving, we approached her and spoke with her. As a result, we learned that while on holiday, her husband had been taken into hospital and she was visiting him daily. With no idea as to whether she was a believer or not, we promised to pray. Next morning, thinking it would at least help to pass the time for her, I left a copy of *Time to Shine* at the reception, together with my business card. Weeks later, she rang me and told me the book had 'changed her life'.

On another occasion, while on a clifftop showing a visiting friend where Henry Francis Lyte wrote his famous hymn 'Abide With Me', I was approached by a man – a complete stranger – whom I imagine must have overheard our conversation. While my husband and friend walked on, this man told me of his experience at a convent school, where the 'penguins' had rapped his knuckles because he was left-handed. That experience, naturally, had had a negative effect on his view of God and church.

We spoke at length and I learned that his marriage was over, that his wife had 'taken everything', that he had 'nothing', and that he'd always wanted to 'end his days' in Torbay. I left, eventually, to continue sightseeing with my husband and friend, then ran back when I felt that the Holy Spirit was telling me to give this man a copy of *Time to Shine*, which I happened to have in the car. When we returned, later, he was sitting in the back of his van reading.

It was only the following morning when I woke that the significance of his remark hit me. Did 'ending his days in Torbay' mean living there? Or had he been suicidal? Was he standing on that clifftop with intent?

I may never know. But this I do know: I was prompted by God to give that book to this man. And I share this with you now because it is to God's glory that he chose to use me to be his ears and eyes; his hands and feet; his love and compassion.

- How does it make you feel when you hear of the bitterness and emptiness that can encompass the hearts and souls of people in Susan's situation, who feel they've been robbed of meaningful life?
- Do you find it difficult to believe that God is on our side when you read of the terrible suffering in the lives of people like Susan James and Phil Godfrey?
- Or can you see, and applaud, the way in which he confounds the worldly view of success, and uses the weak, the foolish, and the lowly things of this world to bring about his will? Even in changing the way insurance companies look upon those with HIV and AIDS?

GOD'S PURPOSE FOR US?
To shine a light on our story, and thus to glorify God.

29: Ears of Corn Midst Bramble and Thorn

*Consider it pure joy, my brothers and sisters, whenever you face
trials of many kinds, because you know that the testing of your faith
produces perseverance. Let perseverance finish its work so that you
may be mature and complete, not lacking anything.*
(James 1:2–4)

You might think, *Wow! With commissions from Hodder, she's made
it, big time*. And so it would appear. With speaking engagements all
over the country, TV appearances, plus interviews on BBC Radio
York, Radio Manchester, Radio Devon, and Dorset, nearly an hour
with Anna Raeburn on Talk Radio in London, and a debate on the
eve of the Irish Referendum on divorce, which took place on BBC
Radio Leeds, it certainly felt like it. Told by one presenter that I was
a 'natural' I realised that as an introvert I was in my element in the
studio, with no sense of the hundreds, even thousands, who might
be tuning in to hear me. During phone-in periods, I would close
my eyes so I could imagine my caller and feel I was speaking to that
person face to face. In every way, I felt affirmed in my calling to be
a writer and speaker.

I was invited out for lunch in London, first with one of the
HarperCollins' editors, then with one from Hodder to discuss the
possibility of further books. The latter, I learned, was in respect of
a lady who had sustained massive injury due to a fall from a horse
and, having read *Healed Within*, now wanted to share her story.

A delightful woman, when I visited her in her Devon home, she
told me how, having come to faith, she had been determined to
overcome her infirmities. So, fed up with having to use a bedpan,
she had staggered from her bed to the bathroom. But once there,
she had no idea which receptacle to use and, hoisting herself onto
the washbasin, had proceeded to use that as a toilet. She laughed,

and I joined with her. There were issues between her and her husband, however, and when it came to the point of signing the contract for Hodder she backed out. He, it appeared, did not want the embarrassment as he was about to be knighted by Her Majesty.

Meanwhile, other matters had taken over. The joy of Vicky having overcome her addiction and being settled in Wales had been matched by the delight in seeing Sarah give birth to our first grandson. Conversely, in the same year, Pete had had to endure the loss of his father. While I was made to face one of my worst fears.

'I'd like to leave teaching and start a business,' Pete said to me one day.

My heart sank. I knew things had been difficult for him for a while, when a parent had incited others against him saying he was unable to maintain discipline in class. But the thought of my darling, gentle husband running a business? Noooo!

'You know it's the last thing I want, after all I went through with James,' I replied, as mildly as I could.

Pete looked down, unable to meet my gaze.

'I know. I hate doing this to you. But my parents were business people. And it's something I've always wanted to do.'

How could I refuse him? I'd had my dreams fulfilled by the Lord. How could I now deny Pete his – especially given the support he'd given me?

And so it was that he left teaching – midst an outcry of sorrow from the very parents who had previously berated him – and took on a franchise in which he became the distributor for a particular brand of greetings cards all over Devon and Cornwall.

Not long afterwards, I ended up in hospital. Again. And again. The problem was intense pain in my upper abdomen. Occurring invariably at night, Pete became convinced I must be having a heart attack. As were the ambulance crew when they came to take me into A&E. Repeatedly they would give me an ECG, attaching electrodes to my chest, back and front, but no diagnosis was ever reached. After a night or so in hospital, Pete would collect me and take me home – only for the whole procedure to occur again within a matter of months.

Eventually, cottoning on to the fact that I had been prescribed laxatives throughout my entire life, my doctor sent me to see a gastroenterologist, then a colorectal surgeon. Following various procedures at different hospitals over a period of time, I finally had a diagnosis. One of the scans showed that the radio-active pills I had been required to swallow were stuck in my transverse colon, showing that I had no peristalsis in that region. In other words, everything stopped moving at that point because of the absence of ganglion – tiny finger-like nerves designed to send messages to the brain and thus activate the muscles of the intestines. As if that were not enough, it appeared that I also had an overlong, knotted small intestine, plus a megacolon.

Everything now made sense! The medical name for such a condition was Hirschsprung. A congenital abnormality, it was normally detected at birth and duly corrected with surgery, a pull-through procedure whereby the faulty section was removed. I reasoned that because of the time and place of my birth in a remote part of Scotland during the war, it had been overlooked. Now, however, I was told that surgery would be required and so a date for my operation was fixed.

Because of my persistent back and bowel problems, I had retained the private medical insurance I'd had when married to James. As a single parent having persistent surgical procedures, it had made sense to do so, I reasoned. And when I'd changed banks, on marrying Pete, and had been talked into switching to their medical insurance, I'd had no hesitation in doing so.

All was set. My bags were packed. The required fluids-only diet had been followed. Surgery was booked for 9.30 next morning. Despite previous gynaecological operations, it was only natural that I should feel tense. The recovery period would be lengthy, and Pete would have to continue working.

At 7.30 p.m. the phone rang. My operation, I learned, had been cancelled. Falsely accused of having concealed my condition when switching my medical insurance, I learned that my policy was deemed invalid. Devastated, I wept uncontrollably until friends, summoned by Pete, came to pray with me. Useless? You bet! A misfit? Oh, yes! A waste of space? Why had God let me born? Why indeed?

I struggled on. If healing in this respect was a non-event, however, I was soon to find that God had not abandoned me. When a lady whom I'd helped to come to faith revealed that she had a medical problem, I took her to a healing seminar in Exeter. Following Colin Urquhart's talk, he invited those with a need for healing to stand, and for those alongside to lay hands on them whilst he prayed. Working upwards from the feet, he prayed for each part of the body individually as different people stood, and my friend duly received healing for her shoulder complaint.

When all areas of the body had been covered in prayer, Colin hesitated.

'There's someone here with a medical problem that hasn't been covered,' he said. 'Please stand if that is you.'

No one stood. He continued, describing, little by little, a specific condition and its whereabouts on the body.

'I want you to come up here, on stage, and allow me to pray for you personally,' he finished.

I felt myself going hot and cold. I'd been diagnosed with a skin condition – follicular mucinosis – some months earlier. Having spoken to my cousin's husband, a dermatologist who worked for the World Health Organisation, I'd been told that there was no known cure so I'd held out no hope of healing. But the thought of going up on stage in front of hundreds of people appalled me.

Reverend Urquhart would not give up! He'd clearly had a vision, and when his description became so specific that I could not ignore it, I went up on stage, was prayed for and, within days, was healed of the complaint.

As if that were not sufficient a lesson for me, God, it seemed, had yet more plans for me. Having gained weight in recent years, I'd been attending Weight Watchers. Once I reached the desired weight, I was asked if I would consider becoming a leader. This would involve training before leading several groups in a radius of a few miles, followed by regular monthly visits to Headquarters with other group leaders in order to share feedback. Given that Pete's income from his business was not great, it seemed that this was an answer to prayer.

In addition to the WW training, I enlisted in evening classes for public speaking, learning how to project my voice; to make eye-contact; to speak as if to each person in turn rather than simply to the crowd; to invite participation. With several large groups to run, I found myself not only making sufficient money to augment our income in a meaningful way, but also enjoying the reward of helping men and women achieve their potential.

'I've always been this weight,' one lady told me as she stood on the scales.

'Twelve stone?' I replied, moving the weights along the bar. 'Your poor mother must have been in agony delivering you at that weight.'

She laughed with me as she realised her error.

Then I found further evening employment which did not interfere with my writing time. *Weekenders* was the name of an American company specialising in soft cotton jersey clothing for women. In a pre-internet era when party-plan selling was at its zenith, it was an easy way to earn a living. It also opened up opportunities for speaking at Christian groups seeking outreach. The idea was that two or three members of the audience would model the clothes while I demonstrated their versatility with sashes and buckles that could completely change the appearance of each outfit. It wasn't difficult to add a word or two about how we are clothed in the righteousness of God, and this became the fore-runner of an increased speaker's role in my life.

And then, only seven years after he'd left teaching, Pete's business began to unravel. Following a period of economic uncertainty, the UK fell into recession. Several of his clients went to the wall owing us money and, as a result, it looked as if we, too, might go into liquidation. Turning my back on the novel I had written and was about to submit to publishers, I realised that I had to do everything possible to help prevent that scenario. Leaving the franchise, we set up in business on our own. I took over the administration so as to give Pete a better chance of selling, and invested money in a Riso – a professional printing machine. We added the printing of flyers, business stationery and business cards to our services.

Then Ruth, who had enjoyed a gap year working around the world, followed by a teaching degree, decided that she would join the business. Calling on our artistic backgrounds, together she and I began designing and printing a series of cards and notelets. Being in a tourist destination, we built the business up, selling personalised stationery to hotels, bars and restaurants. My pencil drawings, a skill derived from the time when I'd undertaken my interior design course, were titled *Devon Dwellings* and included a potted history of each place, while Ruth, having inherited her father's quirky humour, took a more modern and imaginative approach with the cards she designed.

Once again, as we worked together and attempted to build the business, it appeared that God had his hand on us. Then disaster struck, yet again.

Reflections & questions

Bad things come in threes, so they say. I felt I'd lost count of the number happening to us. It seemed that every time we saw some success, it would be countered with negatives. Yet the Bible tells us again and again to trust in God.

Have I not commanded you? Be strong and courageous. Do not be afraid; do not be discouraged, for the LORD your God will be with you wherever you go.
(Joshua 1:9)

There were friends who told us, afterwards, that I should never have given up writing; that trusting in God meant just that: soldiering on as we were. That may be. But I knew I could never have lived with myself if I'd denied Pete first the opportunity to leave teaching and start his business; second to have left him to fend for himself in the face of recession and the threat of bankruptcy. No, I don't understand to this day why it happened as it did. Be that as it may, I know I would take the same decision again were it to happen today. He had loved and supported me throughout my writing career to date. How could I fail to reciprocate?

The point is that, once again, I learned that God's *purpose* for his children does not necessarily lie in one particular type of skill, pursuit, or career. It fills them all. This is not about *doing*, but about *being*. Our purpose might thus be described not so much in terms of ministry we might take up, but much more to do with who we are: with perception and discernment; with seeing and seeking opportunities to bring God's love and encouragement to those for whom he died, in whatever circumstance presents itself. Brambles and weeds may threaten the growth of what he has planted in us; but if we put our trust in him, if our faith and perseverance become the food by which we're nurtured, then it may be that we grow all the stronger as a result. Only then will we know the truth that:

> *The grasslands of the wilderness become a lush pasture, and the hillsides blossom with joy.* (Psalm 65:12 NLT)

- What trials and temptations have you faced, and have they threatened to choke you, like thorns, or have you been strengthened in perseverance?
- Have you ever had to make a choice between turning away from what you believed to be the 'promised land' and giving up on your dreams in order to 'do the right thing'? How did that manifest itself? A vision? A Word? Or just plain instinct?
- Has doing so released other gifts you'd either forgotten about – as with Ruth and me with our artistic skills – or new ones such as my speaking?

GOD'S PURPOSE FOR US?
To trust in God's healing when it comes, but to accept that he may have other plans for us when it is withheld.

30: Pips of Truth Beneath the Peel

For our light and momentary troubles are achieving for us an eternal glory that far outweighs them all. So we fix our eyes not on what is seen, but on what is unseen, since what is seen is temporary, but what is unseen is eternal.
(2 Corinthians 4:17–18)

Despite the long hours spent building up the business, the year behind us had been filled with pleasure and success. In addition to all the TV and radio broadcasts I'd been asked to undertake, I'd been interviewed live at the Princess Theatre in Torquay by Steve Chalke. Once again I learned that speaking – even before fifteen hundred people – didn't faze me. Put me among them and I'd be lost. But there on the stage I felt privileged to be sharing my testimony. Likewise, when I spoke to seven hundred people in Bournemouth.

Family life had been equally rewarding. Vicky, despite a distrust of men acquired whilst on drugs, had settled down with her boyfriend and was still living in Wales. She'd refused to accept his proposal of marriage, but they'd had a baby boy, our third grandchild since the birth of Sarah's second son. Their visit to us, soon afterwards, had caused us to rethink aspects of our faith.

'Do we put them in separate bedrooms?' I asked Pete, a frown on my face. 'Or do we accept that they're together?'

I had never hidden my Christian principles from my children so they knew exactly where we stood on such things. Vicky had shared with me her forebodings about marriage and her distrust of men. She'd witnessed what had happened between her father and me, but more than that she'd seen for herself, as a drug-addict, how manipulative and controlling some males could be with women. Again she assured me that she'd never sold herself or allowed others to have control over her body.

Her refusal to marry was understandable, but were we now to adhere to what Scripture had to say about sexual relationships outside marriage, or should we capitulate to her feelings?

'It seems a bit daft to put them in separate rooms,' Pete agreed. 'I mean, they've had a baby together. What's the point of standing on principle?'

We talked and prayed some more and came to the conclusion that, despite the absence of a wedding service, they were one flesh in God's eyes. Surely, we concurred, it would be better to show God's love rather than adhere to laws already broken.

That decision spoke more to Vicky than any other. Tears filled her eyes when I told her that I'd put a cot in the double bedroom next to ours, ready for the three of them.

'I do believe,' she said to me earnestly. 'I really do.'

Memories of the vision I'd had when Sarah had been baptised filled my heart: my three girls paddling at the water's edge and being lifted to safety by the hand of God.

More than a year later, awaking one summer morning to a cup of tea in bed, a card and a beautiful bouquet of flowers, how could I help but smile at the good fortune God had brought to my life? Pete and I had plans to celebrate our twelfth wedding anniversary that day: twelve of the happiest years we had either of us known. In addition to the intimacy shared in marriage, we enjoyed a 'best-friendship' in which we had nothing to hide from one another. We felt truly blessed.

So when the phone rang later that morning as we opened our anniversary cards, the last thing I expected was that the bloom of joy would be wrenched from our hearts and trampled upon. The caller was my eldest daughter, Sarah. She'd just returned from a doctor's appointment.

'Mom,' her voice broke as she told me the reason for her call.

Her GP, she learned, had been called out to investigate a suspicious death. What Sarah hadn't envisaged was that it was her sister. Vicky, it transpired, had been to a barbecue the previous evening. She'd then been found dead that morning, with her baby in the cot beside her.

The world fell in on me. Darkness descended. Cries of anguish were wrenched from my throat.

I remember little of what followed. Pete packed a case for the two of us and we set off on the six- or seven-hour journey to North Wales. Sarah's sons, now aged three and four, announced, on our arrival:

'Vicky gone to be with the Lord Jesus, Grandma.'

We went to the undertakers and were invited to see Vicky's body. She looked grey and vacant; nothing of the sunny little moon-face remained.

'You can touch her. Kiss her if you want,' I was told.

Did I want to? No! I did not.

'That's not my daughter,' I said.

A stunned silence ensued. Clearly the undertaker thought there was an error.

'It's her body,' I explained. 'But it's not her.'

Vicky's baby was being cared for by a friend, and the house was a crime scene until the police completed their search. At which point, a day or so later, we were allowed to go in to collect Vicky's belongings. We were not the only ones! Following us there seemed to be a steady stream of people. We gathered everything together, but I became aware of things that were missing. A day or so later, the police announced that a pack of morphine tablets had been found on the mantelpiece; that the local surgery had been broken into; and that it had come from there.

Positive that it had not been there when we'd first entered the house, I asked the police what this meant? They admitted they had not found the drugs during their earlier search. As to what lay behind Vicky's death, there were to be no answers until a post mortem had been undertaken.

A fortnight later, the pathology report arrived. The cause of Vicky's death was stated as being asphyxiation due to vomiting as a result of ingesting a single morphine tablet. And at the bottom of page one it said: *a known drug addict*.

'A known drug addict?' I said at the police station, my voice breaking. 'She's been off drugs for five years.'

Vicky's funeral took place in the local church, with standing room only. At her father's request, Sarah read Alfred Lord Tennyson's moving poem, *Crossing the Bar*.

Sunset and evening star,
And one clear call for me!
And may there be no moaning of the bar,
When I put out to sea,

But such a tide as moving seems asleep,
Too full for sound and foam,
When that which drew from out the boundless deep
Turns again home.

Twilight and evening bell,
And after that the dark!
And may there be no sadness of farewell,
When I embark;

For tho' from out our bourne of Time and Place
The flood may bear me far,
I hope to see my Pilot face to face
When I have crost the bar.

Jokes abounded, with James' friends, about the drinks that would later be lined up in the pub bar, while I wondered whether Vicky, having crossed the bar, had met her Pilot face to face? I believed she probably had.

'How could God let this happen when we've prayed for Vicky for so long,' a lady from my church wept with me on our return home. A relatively new Christian, she had been in my nurture group following Mission England and was clearly devastated. Her response reminded me of so much that my father had said in the past about what he saw as the absence of God's love.

'Rita,' I replied, taking her hands in mine. 'I believe this was a set-up job.'

Briefly, I explained that Vicky had begged me to write an article for a well-known magazine, telling her story in an effort to encourage others in their attempt to give up drugs. I'd agreed to do so on condition that Vicky was not identified.

'You don't want to be targeted by drug-pushers,' I'd said to her.

True to herself, Vicky thought otherwise. She was proud of her achievements. She even spoke about training to help other addicts. So the photograph that was published alongside my article was of her, full face.

'I think someone was trying to get her back on drugs so she would become a supplier,' I told Rita.

And suddenly, I recalled a phone call I'd received from Vicky, in which she'd told me only a week before she died that she was fed up with the pressure people were putting on her. I'd asked her to explain and she'd become quite upset, but she wouldn't elucidate, telling me not to worry.

'She had a list of her London "friends" in a little black book,' I continued. 'That book is missing. If whoever slipped that morphine tablet into her drink at the barbecue had succeeded in making her dependent again in the hope of getting her to be a supplier, then I believe it would have been a fate worse than death. It would have been hell on earth. For her. For her baby. For us. For her partner and friends. I believe God knew that, and took her to be with him.'

The explanation I gave to Rita was without forethought. Indeed, it felt like a truth revealed to me: as if the Holy Spirit were speaking through me. To me!

The Inquest, at which we were told only James would be permitted to speak, was to follow weeks later. Meanwhile, determined that my daughter would not be written off as *a known drug addict*, I spent my time piecing together evidence that he might share during the proceedings. For a start, Vicky had been to our local dentist during a recent visit to us. Having been attending the same practice for years, we were well known, but the dental nurse's glove had split while she was attending to Vicky. Knowing her background, she'd asked for Vicky to have blood tests, terrified that she might be HIV+.

I met with James to discuss my findings. Together we united behind the statements I'd gathered together to prove Vicky's innocence. No way was she a *a known drug addict*.

The day of the hearing came. I sat and listened to what those who had been with Vicky in the days and hours before her death had to say. Then it was James' turn to speak. Sadly, clearly overwhelmed, his stutter made it almost impossible to hear or to follow what he was saying. While I felt every sympathy for him, I would not – could not – let this stand. Flouting the instructions from the Coroner, in which I was forbidden to speak, I stood and made clear my findings. Uninvited, I told him and a full courtroom what I had learned.

Vicky's recent tests had shown, conclusively, not only that she was clear of HIV but, also, of drugs. As had other tests she'd requested from her own doctor in Wales, both when she was pregnant and, more recently, when she'd been suffering from severe abdominal pain. Likewise, her driving licence had depended upon six-monthly tests taken on behalf of the DVLA. There were no drugs in her system! And no indication of her having taken any.

All this evidence appeared to have been concealed until I brought it to light. Despite this, in a puzzling move by the Coroner, all other witnesses were instructed to say nothing that might incriminate them, or others, and thus lead to a Crown Prosecution. He agreed only to change the wording on Vicky's death certificate to Accidental.

We then learned more. It appeared that the police had been watching the premises for some time. Before Vicky had moved in! They'd arrested two local people but had not charged them. They pressed us to take out a private prosecution. It was clear that there had been some sort of cover up. Nonetheless, after much prayer on Pete's and my part and discussion with James, we decided to take it no further but to leave judgement and justice to God.

Reflections & questions

Vicky's death was twenty-four years ago but I have never truly 'got over it'. As Prince William and Prince Harry admitted recently, when speaking of the loss of their mother, the shock is as real today as it was then. Tears catch me out regularly. No mother expects to lose her child. And while Vicky was adult when she died, the natural expectation is always that a daughter will outlive her mother. It's a given.

One thing I learned, above all, is the difficulty others appear to have when faced with those who grieve. Most people, I found, tend to turn away; to walk on the other side of the street so as to avoid having to engage in conversation. Just as with mental illness or physical disability, this is an issue that needs to be addressed. Knowing the embarrassment grief affords those looking on, the tendency is for us to believe that we should grieve alone. Again, as the Princes showed, a sorrow shared is not a sorrow halved. But in its sharing, it is a sorrow of benefit to others!

Another lesson I learned, and was invited to share on American radio stations is the tendency for self-blame and depression. *Could I have done something to prevent Vicky's death*, I continue to ask myself? Could I have done more when she was a child? Had I been a better mother then, might she, perhaps, have led a longer and more fulfilling life? Never been caught up in the world of addiction? Never been targeted by those wanting her to supply for them?

No matter how much we might attempt to follow Pauline Gates' advice to let the head knowledge we have about God's love and forgiveness for us drop eighteen inches and inhabit our hearts, the reality, I find, is that even if I achieve that aim, it doesn't last. Jeff Lucas is right to say that we need to monitor and control that internal dialogue. But he is right, too, in admitting that it is not an easy thing to do. If we're honest, we have to accept the simple fact that leaning on God is an ongoing, never-ending practice.

The LORD is a refuge for the oppressed, a stronghold in times of trouble. Those who know your name trust in you, for you, LORD, have never forsaken those who seek you.
(Psalm 9:9–10)

- If you were faced with the death of a loved one in suspicious circumstances, would you have followed through with a private prosecution in an attempt to get to the truth?
- Have you experienced guilt and self-blame following the death of a loved one? If so, how did you go about rectifying those damaging thoughts? Or did you see them as punishment?

GOD'S PURPOSE FOR US?
The Bible tells us to love the sinner while hating the sin, which must mean that there are times when it is right to give precedence to demonstrating God's love rather than standing on Christian principle.

The Fruit of Forgiveness
1995 Onwards

31: Give and Take

The LORD gave and the LORD has taken away; may the name of the
LORD be praised.
(Job 1:21)

We are told that life and death are the only certainties we can ever know, and so it would seem. Only months after Vicky's death, Pete's brother succumbed to a brain haemorrhage.

Soon afterwards, I was interviewed on the BBC *Songs of Praise* by Pam Rhodes. I confess I didn't find it easy being filmed walking side by side on the narrow paths around the lakes in Cockington – a medieval village – whilst sharing my story of Vicky. But with several retakes and a patient cameraman we got there eventually. Having previously made a Victoria sponge cake for the researcher, a chocolate cake for the cameraman and a fruit cake for the producer – each of whom had visited me separately in the weeks before the programme – I produced a banana ice-cream cake for Pam when she came home with me for tea after filming.

'I knew there had to be a cake in it somewhere,' she laughed, and she rang me the following week for the recipe.

Not long after, I was taken on by the Tessa Sayle Literary Agency, who once represented Britain's bestselling novelist, Mary Wesley CBE. As a result, I continued to receive requests from Hodder, then from HarperCollins. But eventually, invited to meet the Senior Editor for lunch with a view to discussing a particular writing commission, I had to decline because, with the pressure of work, my ability to meet deadlines was too unreliable. It hurt! But the fact was that although God had answered our prayers in that Pete's business had settled down, it was generating insufficient income to keep us.

A short time later, I was offered what I took to be another God-given opportunity. David Peacock, our house group leader for many years, and Company Secretary for Jubilate Hymns, knew of our predicament. Founded by Bishop Michael Baughen in the 1960s, the company comprised some eighty writers and composers of a couple of thousand hymns, music and worship songs written in contemporary language, producing books that included *Hymns for Today's Church*, *Youth Praise*, *Psalm Praise*, and later, *Church Family Worship*.

'The Copyright and Financial Manager of Jubilate is about to retire,' said David. 'Would you be interested in taking it on?'

Having mastered the technology of a fax machine when married to James, plus Alan Sugar's Amstrad, followed by a desktop computer on which I'd run the administrative and financial matters of Pete's business for so long, I had no hesitation in accepting. Nevertheless, there was one important issue that had to be faced.

'I'll have to have a new dress,' I said to Pete, 'I'm going to be meeting with the directors in London and some of them are bishops!'

Robed in my newly acquired navy-and-white silk frock, which I'd purchased in the sales, I attended my first meeting at St Paul's in Robert Adam Street. Present were David Peacock, Head of Music and Worship at London School of Theology; Michael Saward, Canon Treasurer at St Paul's Cathedral; Noël Tredinnick, Director of Music at All Souls, Langham Place; and others, all of whom were dressed casually. But it was Michael Baughen, Bishop of Chester, who most impressed me in his baseball cap and trainers. Like the greaseproof-paper package hidden in my thirteenth birthday cake, I got the message loud and clear! As in 2 Corinthians 10:7, it was not outward appearances that mattered, but what was inside.

If only such clarity had existed within my family. Pete, Ruth and I were invited for lunch with my parents, one day soon afterwards, while my middle sister, Gilly, was visiting. My mother, to my great surprise, insisted after the meal that we leave the washing-up and, instead, led us all into the lounge.

'Your father has something he wants to say.' She seated herself and looked to him to begin.

Standing at the window of the house they had built all those years ago, I gazed with pleasure at the large garden that surrounded it: the sloping front lawn which gave way to a view of the bay, the mouth of the estuary, and the open sea beyond. Then I turned, raised an eyebrow in Gilly's direction, and took a seat.

The proposition put to us that afternoon hinged on the fact that my father had health issues with a prognosis of only two years to live. Concerned that my mother might not have sufficient income following his death, he had been looking into equity release on the house. We then learned that a suggestion had been put forward, whereby my youngest sister and her husband should purchase my parents' house and care for my mother on my father's death.

'What,' asked my father, 'are your views on that?'

A stunned silence ensued, followed by requests for further information and the raising of some legitimate concerns from Gilly and me.

'What happens if the doctors are wrong and Mum goes first?' I asked.

That possibility, it seemed, had not been considered.

'Or supposing she needs nursing care?'

Each enquiry seemed only to infuriate my father.

'Well, if you've made up your minds . . .' we ventured.

His anger escalated. 'We want your opinion, your approval,' he roared.

Had they considered other options, we asked, putting forward alternatives.

'Well you wouldn't want the house,' said my mother. 'Pete couldn't run his business from here.'

Confused, I shook my head. 'Who says I wouldn't want it? Pete could run his business anywhere,' I protested.

Accused of jealousy and hypocrisy, I fell silent. It seemed, however, that I was in a no-win situation. Vilified for whatever I said, my silence then brought forth accusations of sulking. What's more, I suddenly remembered previous conversations with my mother concerning the supposition that I wouldn't want the house.

'So that's what it was about,' I muttered, unaware until it was too late that I'd been overheard.

Once again, I was subjected to a furious onslaught: unfounded accusations of resentment and greed.

The disintegration of once loving relationships was beyond anything I could ever have imagined. When requests from me to discuss things with my youngest sister, Kat, met with resistance on all sides, it was clear that far from being a proposal open to discussion, a hard and fast decision had, in fact, been reached. I returned home in floods of tears.

Reflections & questions

It's tempting, sometimes, to feel that God gives with one hand and takes with the other. We're told that Job, a wealthy man with an affectionate family who met regularly to celebrate birthdays together, was known as *the greatest man among all the peoples of the East.* Yet despite his allegiance to God, Satan had his eye upon him. Putting his faith to the test, he sent disaster upon disaster upon him until, finally, the worst happened.

> *While he* (a messenger) *was still speaking, yet another messenger came and said, 'Your sons and daughters were feasting and drinking wine at the eldest brother's house, when suddenly a mighty wind swept in from the desert and struck the four corners of the house. It collapsed on them and they are dead, and I am the only one who has escaped to tell you!'*
>
> *At this, Job got up and tore his robe and shaved his head. Then he fell to the ground in worship and said: 'Naked I came from my mother's womb, and naked I shall depart. The Lord gave and the Lord has taken away; may the name of the Lord be praised.'*
>
> *In all this, Job did not sin by charging God with wrongdoing.*
> (Job 1:18–22)

God, in his love and mercy, had given me a job and redeemed Pete's and my financial security. Yet I'd been robbed of my family and my peace of mind. In spite of that, like Job, I could not lay what had happened to me at the feet of the Lord. Once again, self-recrimination flooded through my being. At the same time, I recognised that I'd been misunderstood. Misinterpreted. Despite the ongoing accusations of jealousy and greed, I knew that all I wanted was reconciliation with my family.

- Are you ever tempted to think that God doesn't care? That he has the power to prevent or redeem a situation but fails to do so?
- What experiences have you encountered that made you feel like this? How did they work out in the end: positively, or negatively?
- What relationships do you have in your life that require reconciliation? Are you able to face up to them?

GOD'S PURPOSE FOR US?
Like Job, we are to accept that everything we have in this world came about at God's hand, and that he owes us nothing.

32: Dying to Self

*Very truly I tell you, unless a grain of wheat falls to the ground and
dies, it remains only a single seed. But if it dies, it produces many
seeds.*
(John 12:24)

Being part of the Jubilate team was a life-saver in every sense.
They were a lovely bunch of people and I felt instantly at ease. This
being before the days of Christian Copyright Licensing being used
universally, I worked from home in our purpose-built conservatory
office, liaising worldwide with individuals, churches and other
organisations, including the BBC. Issuing licences for the use of more
than two thousand Jubilate works of words and music, collecting,
allocating and distributing large sums of royalties and fees, I was in
charge of the general running of the company. When we partnered
with George Shorney of Hope Publishing in the USA, Jubilate works
found their way into American hymnals, and vice versa.

With regular directors' meetings in London, some of them at St
Paul's Cathedral when Michael Saward became Chairman, I soon
made friends with everyone. Events at the Christian Copyright
Licensing offices in Eastbourne, or in Holland which composer
David Iliff and I attended, were an added bonus. As was Prom Praise
led by Noël Tredinnick at the Royal Albert Hall, when Pete and I
were given seats next to the Royal Box, and on another occasion, a
commemorative meal with everyone at St Katherine's Dock.

Nevertheless, despite the financial stability God had secured for
us, I still yearned to write again. With the maxim he had given me
to 'comfort others with the comfort I had received' I never felt truly
at peace.

Comforting others was a lesson Sarah, too, had learned. Married to a farmer and living in North Wales, she was fully cognisant of the issues raised by the foot-and-mouth crisis of 2001. With the trauma rendering some farmers suicidal, she duly set up a telephone helpline and assisted many in reaching a point of resolution. Word spread and, as a result, friends persuaded her to train for ministry. If ever there was an answer to prayer that surely was. At her ordination, I had the privilege of sharing the story of her near-death experience in infancy, my plea to God to save her and my promise to bring her up to know and love him.

How good is God! That same year, Ruth married a charming young man she'd met through friends. Once again, James featured in our lives; first in performing his parental duty in giving Ruth away, then via his persistent phone calls to me over the next couple of years, on the pretext of having lost her telephone number.

Ringing one day, ostensibly to speak to me about Vicky's son's inheritance since her demise, I learned that it was, in fact, to tell me he had been given only months to live. With Pete listening in, he begged me to come to his funeral and told me that Sarah had agreed to co-lead the service.

We had long since reached a place of forgiveness and reconciliation. Shortly before he died, I sat at his hospital bedside, held his hand and prayed with him. United as a family, we gathered together for his funeral. Using the skills she'd acquired while working for Pete's business, Ruth adorned the Order of Service with one of Vicky's drawings, while Sarah, once again, read James' favourite poem, *Crossing the Bar*.

My Christmas letter in 2003 gives ample reflection of what occurred:

The most recent event of the year – the death of Sarah's and Ruth's father – vividly demonstrates how crucial it is to maintain a duality of vision: the ability to see things as they are, but also to see the good in them. It was clear when we last saw James (while we watched the Red Arrows) *that he was in a bad way and we were shocked to see how frail and yellow he had become. His sense of humour, however, remained intact. Responding to a comment on the nattiness of his walking stick (a series of perforated metal tubes that pulled apart to add/reduce its length) he complained that 'it wasn't much good because, although he kept filling it, the gin leaked out of the holes'!*

Within weeks he was in Derriford Hospital. The girls feared the worst but, in fact, those five weeks proved invaluable. Sarah came down and, between the three of us visiting his bedside, we had more time alone, more opportunity, and more 'meaningful' conversations with James than any of us had managed to have during the preceding twenty-five years! Fortunately, in Pete I have a loving and understanding husband, who was well able to empathise with my sadness on James' death when it occurred on 26th October.

Ruth, meanwhile, despite our prayers, had all but given up on the possibility of starting a family.

'I'm not going down the IVF route,' she told me. 'If God wants me to have a baby he'll give me one.'

He did! Not one, but two. Nine months and two days after her father's death she had twins: a boy and a girl. Her faith was rewarded. Our joy was complete.

In 2004, seven years after I began working for Jubilate, Pete sold his business and we job shared for a further seven years. During that time, we had the privilege of being invited to occupy Michael and Jackie Saward's apartment at Tobacco Dock in Wapping while they were away on holiday. It just happened that it was the week of 7/7 when, as an act of terrorism, a series of suicide bomb attacks hit London's transport system. Determined not to give in to such threats, and despite pleas from the family, we went up to Paddington by train and crossed London by bus rather than on the Underground. A wonderful week followed, including a visit to the Tower of London plus a river trip to Greenwich.

Still I missed writing! Nonetheless, if ever I was in doubt about my calling 'to comfort others with the comfort I'd received', God was about to reaffirm it. Early that summer I was called for my first (and last) Jury Service. I went with a sense of expectation that God could and would use me and, in no time, I ascertained that there was another Christian among the twelve.

To say that the case was harrowing would be an understatement. It included pornography, paedophilia and rape, one defendant and numerous victims – small boys who gave evidence via a video link, plus young men with speech impediments and other learning difficulties. The offences had been going on, unchecked, for more than forty years. With a jury made up of four men my age, and six of the other seven women in their twenties and thirties, it came as a shock to me to discover how strongly opinionated a minority could be, and how much of the evidence recalled by others I had missed. I began to feel depressed. Old and useless. Unable to see any purpose in my being there. And ashamed to think I had ever believed I could make a difference.

Over the weeks, however, all that was to change. Four of the younger women and I travelled daily by train to Exeter. Bonds began to be formed. When there was a cut finger, an irritating cough, or tears in the jury room, I found that I had the necessary plaster, throat pastille, or tissue in my big black handbag, together with a hand to squeeze or a shoulder to cry on. My fellow jurors began, affectionately, to call me Mary Poppins – a small dint in my street cred. Yet, though humbling to discover that I wasn't being called upon for my intellectual prowess (such as it may, or may not be!) but simply for whatever human compassion and understanding I had to offer, it was also uplifting.

The trial continued for months, concluding with two days of debate. Unanimous in bringing guilty verdicts on all twenty-one specimen counts of paedophilia, the rape case saw us divided. Finally, God allowed me to have my say, to the point where I was asked to be the speaker for the jury, a position I declined in favour of one of the men. When a guilty verdict was brought on that case too, the prosecuting barrister mouthed his thanks to us, and an as yet unidentified young man whom we were later told was the victim, broke down in tears of anguish, reducing us, the jury, to weep with him. Further tears followed when we parted at the end of the trial plus requests from 'my girls' for a reunion.

God had had his way! What's more, he had again shown me the diversity of my calling. He had picked me not simply to bear fruit through my writing, but to give shade and shelter to fellow jurors in need; to bring zest and flavour to our debate; to ensure justice for the final victim. I followed up with letters to the Judge and to CARE (Christian Action, Research and Education) and was delighted to receive a telephoned response from Lyndon Bowring, himself!

Reflections & questions

If handing over my first marriage to God had been hard, doing so with my writing proved harder still. Despite my determination to walk alongside Pete, and my gratitude to God for enabling this via my employment with Jubilate, I felt as if a huge part of me had died. Having to turn down commissions from some of the big publishing companies, and with no time even to write magazine articles felt, to me, as if I were cutting off my hands and feet, tongue and lungs. Without a voice, I felt useless. Without my writing, I felt the arms of death engulf me.

Yet it seemed that in my daughters I saw seeds sown. Ruth's support for me following the falling out with my parents – an event at which she was present – was invaluable. As was the love and help she and Sarah shared in the deaths of their sister and father. With Sarah going into ministry and Ruth about to produce twins, how could I doubt that this was the fulfilment of God's promise to multiply the seed he had sown in me? Hadn't Jesus said, clearly, that we are to relinquish all that we hold dear in order for him to achieve in us the fruitfulness he desires.

Then he called the crowd to him along with his disciples and said: 'Whoever wants to be my disciple must deny themselves and take up their cross and follow me. For whoever wants to save their life will lose it, but whoever loses their life for me and for the gospel will save it. What good is it for someone to gain the whole world, yet forfeit their soul? Or what can anyone give in exchange for their soul? If anyone is ashamed of me and my words in this adulterous and sinful generation, the Son of Man will be ashamed of them when he comes in his Father's glory with the holy angels.'
(Mark 8:34–38)

We see, in Jesus himself, that he laid aside his life, died to the preaching and teaching ministry at which he was so adept, gave up on the gift of healing at which he excelled. And he did it all so that he might die – literally and physically – on the cross. In doing so, he bore fruit. And that fruit, borne as a result of his death, was to bring life and healing to us all; redemption and salvation; hope in a life to come. Like the ear of wheat falling to the ground, the seeds that brought about the life of the church – countless individuals for over two thousand years – were produced, and continue to be produced. But that's not to say that he did so without feeling the pain of his sacrifice. Needing the support of his disciples, he clearly felt the anguish of being let down when they fell asleep in the Garden of Gethsemane. In asking his Father that the cup be taken from him, and in crying out on the cross because he felt forsaken, Jesus makes plain the torment he feels.

I can hardly compare my sacrifice of a writing career with the torture he endured. Yet in sharing his pain with us, Jesus' understanding of our plight, our emotions, is unmistakable. We are not alone. He knows how we feel. He's been there. Done it. There is no shame in being honest.

- What fruitful answers to prayer have you seen, such as mine when, in asking for God's healing of Sarah, I had the joy of seeing her led to becoming ordained?
- How have you been able to relate dying to self with forgiveness of those who have wronged you – and thus known reconciliation as my children and I did with their father?
- What events, like my jury time, have you participated in at which you initially felt yourself to be useless – only to find that God used you in different ways to your expectations?
- What is the hardest thing you've ever been called to give up? How did you respond to such sacrifice? And do you live with regret? Or with a sense of peace, having done God's will, even if you see no positive results as yet?

GOD'S PURPOSE FOR US?
We are to learn that in dying to self, we live in Jesus; that he rewards the righteous, and that those who do harm will reap the consequences.

33: The Free Fruit of Forgiveness

It is for freedom that Christ has set us free. Stand firm, then, and do not let yourselves be burdened again by a yoke of slavery.
(Galatians 5:1)

As it happened, despite the doctor's prognosis of my father's imminent death, he lived on for a further fourteen years. Throughout that time, even though the vitriol and family rift continued, Pete and I sustained a relationship with my parents. In addition to visits to one another for meals, we happily gave them all the help they required, especially during their frequent and lengthy holidays abroad. Picking, blanching and freezing the fruit from the large garden which was now owned by my sister and brother-in-law, dealing with their mail, paying bills and banking cheques where necessary was the easy part. Mowing the lawns back and front, both on a slope at the bottom of the valley, was less so especially when our mower broke down irreparably.

Harder still were periods when accidents or illness necessitated our intervention. At one time it might be a broken limb such as when my father had a fall in the garden, or Mum's heart attack, broken pelvis, or bowel cancer. On a trip to Monte Carlo, one of them was hospitalised and had to be cared for on their return; and on another occasion, my mother, feisty and stubborn as any weed known to gardeners, booked a bridge holiday in Turkey against all advice. Gilly, having been there, described the facilities away from the resorts as less than desirable for two elderly people, so it was an anxious time for all when, within days of arrival, I had a phone call alerting me to the fact that Mum had been knocked over in the foyer and taken to hospital. My father, alone in the hotel until a bed was found for him in the hospital, was distraught.

When the time came for Mum to be released, she was greatly distressed to learn that she would be detained until she could pay her hospital bill. Having forgotten her PIN on the one credit card in her possession, and with my father having mixed up the combination lock on the safe in their room, they were unable to access any other. It fell to me, therefore, to pay the £900 on my card. With a second period in hospital resulting in missed flights, there followed a particularly distressing period when my mother, in several phone calls home, was convinced she was going to die out there. She survived, flew home and promptly fell down the steps of the golf club.

Sadly, despite the effort on our part, there was no compromise when it came to the matter of my parents' house. With Kat and her husband now living and working abroad, Gilly and I were told, incessantly, that they owned it and that we had no option but to accept that. Which we did! Sadly, doing so made no difference to the treatment meted out to me, the eldest. Over the coming years I continued to be subjected to vitriol and persecution for having raised those initial questions. Again and again I sought reconciliation but to no avail. Whenever I broached the subject, the accusations against me came thick and fast. When I refused to speak of it, I was charged with harbouring bitterness. Meanwhile, as time passed, my father became increasingly anxious about finances. Constantly pouring over investments papers, he was in a frenzy.

'At this rate there will be nothing left for your mother when I go.'

It appeared that far from ensuring financial security for Mum, the rent and living costs she and Dad were paying exceeded the return on investment from the sale of the house. Not only that, they were now faced with the fact that, because of its location, its value had soared way beyond the sum they had raised.

Concerned for my father's stress levels as he ranted and raved, I knew I had to do something. But what? Trying to intervene with diplomacy and conciliation, I again met only with resistance and malice.

'Is there any chance you could put a stop to further increases in the rent?' I asked my brother-in-law, having screwed up the courage to ring him.

Only, I was told, if Gilly and I were prepared to give up our inheritance!

Having been denied sight of the sale and rental agreement drawn up by solicitors, I nevertheless found myself constantly piggy in the middle. During one of my sister and brother-in-law's frequent sojourns to the UK, when they would stay at the house, I was told by my parents that Kat and her husband wanted to retire and move in permanently. Mum and Dad, however, wished to adhere to the contract which denied them that right while both parents lived there. A meeting was arranged and I was asked to act as intermediary. It was not a pleasant experience!

Meanwhile, recalling the vitriol my father had poured out for years on those, like myself, who believed in a 'God of love' when he felt the evidence around us showed him to be anything but, I continued to be puzzled as to where he stood. Particularly because, while dealing with his mail when he and Mum were abroad, I discovered that, for years, he'd secretly been sending money to charities supporting children overseas. And then there was the Scripture prize he'd won as a youngster, which had been so instrumental in bringing me to faith. Determined to find out, I approached him one day with the order of service from a friend's funeral.

'You've always said you want a church service when you die,' I began, 'but you've never said which hymns you want.'

We discussed the subject at length then, out of the blue, at what I can only assume was the prompting of the Holy Spirit, I continued:

'Do you know where you're going when you die, Dad?'

In the silence that hung in the air, my mother's face reflected her horror. Then my father pointed heavenward.

'Up there, I hope,' he said, his voice reflecting fervent optimism, plus incredulity that I should dare to ask.

'And does God know?' I responded – again without thought.

'Well, I hope so,' Dad replied. 'I talk to him all the time.'

A sense of peace descended upon me.

Soon afterwards I learned from Kat that my father was suffering from dementia, though his doctor, when I took it up with him, vehemently denied it. Following another fall on my mother's part, I moved down to nurse her. On Kat's return to the UK, she promptly put Dad into a care home. At the end of their leave, when nursing my mother fell to me once more, my brother-in-law phoned from the airport, asked to speak to Pete, and told him that the care home would not keep Dad and that we were to collect him and put him into a secure dementia home. Unable to cope with any more as we were still working, we did so.

'Please don't leave me here,' Dad sobbed, 'I want to go home.'

The anguish and guilt felt by Gilly and me was overwhelming. Yet nothing compared with what was to come.

Three years later, when my father succumbed twice within a month to pneumonia and I talked to the family about palliative care because he was begging to be allowed to 'go', I was reminded of a vision I'd had on waking in bed one morning.

'I see the death of one of my parents as an opportunity to put my arms around Kat, to comfort her, and perhaps to be reconciled,' I'd told Pete.

It almost came to fruition! Reaching out to Kat as we sat and discussed the matter of Dad's end-of-life care with the nursing staff, I did manage to touch her arm and put my hand on her shoulder. A few days later, seated at my father's bedside and with Mum and Kat alongside, I held Dad's hand and sang his favourite hymn aloud:

Dear Lord and Father of mankind, forgive our foolish ways,
Re-clothe us in our rightful mind, in purer lives thy service find,
In deeper reverence, praise. In deeper reverence, praise.

Ten minutes later, on my return home, I learned via a phone call that he had gone. It was, I thought, as if he'd felt released through those words.

Sadly, however, the reconciliation I'd hoped for with Kat escalated into further vitriol. Over the next few years when she and her husband moved into the house, repeated phone calls from Mum's friends – people I'd known for decades – raised similar concerns to those I'd had right from the start.

'What's going on?' they asked, telling me of my mother's tears and distress about events at home.

Again, I was piggy in the middle. Trying – with diplomacy – to smooth things over I would put Mum's case to Kat, who would deal with me only by email. At the same time, I would gently remind Mum that she'd signed up for this, and that when my brother-in-law told her she was a guest in his house, that was, indeed, the case. I was in a no-win situation. Hurtful emails ensued, rendering me an emotional wreck, until Pete wrote and put a stop to them. Increasingly, I felt suicidal.

Things continued to degenerate to the point where Mum asked me to take care of her jewellery and my father's wartime airmail letters, in case they 'disappeared'. It was then that I learned of my label as a 'naughty girl'. And it was then that I learned that, far from having been undiscovered, my intestinal problems, the pain and embarrassment I'd suffered for my entire life, had been well-known at my birth.

'You screamed every time I put you to the breast,' my mother told me, weeping as guilt swept over her. 'Your grandparents and great aunts would have none of it. And even when we took you to have an x-ray when we returned to London, no one would do anything about it.'

Gently, I told her that I didn't blame her. And despite my depression and the urge to end it all, I reminded myself of what God had done in and through my life as a result of my infirmities. The constant pain, the dosing, the embarrassing accidents and hospital visits might dominate my life but, via my writing, he had shown me a way through. That, surely, I told myself, was the prime motive in my having sought 'to comfort others with the comfort I'd received'.

Two years later, things degenerated yet further. Mum came to stay with us over the August Bank Holiday so Kat and her husband could get away.

'They marched me to the bank,' she said.

I couldn't help smiling at the thought of my mother being 'marched' anywhere, but the smile was wiped from my face as she continued. Once there, she said, she was told to sign forms allowing Kat to take over her financial affairs.

'Is this what you want?' the cashier asked of my mother, whom she knew. And when Mum said 'no', she refused to proceed.

Mum's front door key had then been taken from her. Her distress was clear to see. This was her youngest daughter, her favourite daughter, the one to whom she had entrusted her future care. There was worse to come. Towards the end of her visit, I emailed Kat to arrange a time for her return. The response I received told me I was not to take her home, that she was no longer welcome, and that the door would be locked.

Having to consult solicitors, and gain access to my mother's possessions, we were again faced with the possibility of court proceedings. As with Vicky's case, following prayer and discussion, we left judgement in God's hands and took the matter no further.

Reflections
Looking back over my life, I see a pattern of expectation, misconception and frustration. The seeds of expectancy sown by my parents had failed to be met by their perceptions of reality which, in turn, had led to disappointment and aggravation. Hence the writing of my journal in which I saw myself as a failure in all realms of life; a misfit; useless.

It appears, however, that I am not alone. Recent research shows that it is not unusual for eldest children to suffer from depression. The responsibility and expectation placed upon them in childhood can cause internalised self-expectations: namely, that in order to be loved and accepted, they need to meet certain criteria. This was certainly true of me. Until I learned that it was possible to be a reformed perfectionist! Or, at least, one in the making. ☺

Seeking counselling from my good friend and pastor, Andrew Green, I was reminded of the issues of Transactional Analysis in psychology; specifically the Drama Triangle, in which the roles and destructive interaction within a relationship engaged in conflict may be described as: Persecutor, Victim and Rescuer. Accused, constantly, of being the Persecutor by my family, and they the Victim, I could quite see that I'd all too willingly leapt into the role of Rescuer.

'You have to step aside,' Andrew told me. 'Stop allowing yourself to be dragged into the conflict.'

Easier said than done when it's the sister you loved and nurtured from childhood but, with the enlightening Andrew brought me, I did my best. Sadly, despite my prayers and entreaties, there has been no redemption and the pain never entirely goes. God's forgiveness of us sets us free, and so does our forgiveness of others. But it is costly, as Jesus demonstrated in the Garden of Gethsemane and on the cross. When Peter came to Jesus and asked *'Lord, how many times shall I forgive my brother or sister who sins against me?'* he assumed that seven times would be sufficient. He was wrong!

Jesus answered, 'I tell you, not seven times, but seventy-seven times' (Matthew 18:21–22). In doing so, he was implying never-ending forgiveness.

Weeping uncontrollably when David Coffey preached on the subject, I went forward for ministry.

'I've had to shake the dust from my feet as far as my sister is concerned,' I sobbed, quoting Luke 9:5. 'Am I wrong?'

David endorsed my reaction, confirming that forgiveness did not, necessarily, equate to reconciliation, and that I was right to draw a line under the situation. Recalling another verse from the Bible, I reminded myself that although Jesus' forgiveness applied to all, not all were willing to receive it and be reconciled to God. But for those who do, it is vital that we should not doubt it. Despite Pauline Gates' axiom that I should let God's forgiveness of me drop eighteen inches from head to heart, and Stephanie Cole's to leave my sin nailed to the cross, I still weep for my failings whenever I take communion. But my tears are for the one who died for me.

Is this a negative note on which to conclude a book about purpose? I hope not! What is clear to me is that despite all of this, my upbringing, being labelled as a naughty child, my failed marriage, the addiction and ultimate death of my daughter, the persistent acrimony from some members of my family, and the pain of my ongoing health issues, which recently resulted in my being taken into hospital by ambulance six times in twelve months and dominated my life, I have been picked for one purpose only. As have you! That is not to be an outstanding daughter, wife, mother, sister, friend, author or speaker. It is, quite simply, to be part of the body of Jesus; his heart and mind; his eyes and ears; his hands and feet. It is to discern the need of others; to show his love and forgiveness; to shine his light in a dark world; to proclaim his kingdom. As he instructs us:

> *Therefore go and make disciples of all nations, baptising them in the name of the Father and of the Son and of the Holy Spirit, and teaching them to obey everything I have commanded you. And surely I am with you always, to the very end of the age.*
> (Matthew 28:19–20)

The ways in which we do so may vary enormously, as I hope I have demonstrated. Thankfully, as Joshua and Caleb showed on entering the Promised Land, we are never too old to begin. Nor are we alone! Rooted in the true vine that is Jesus, we are joined together, you and I. He is the vine. We are simply the branches that are to bear fruit. And that fruit is to bring glory to him.

THE END

UNHEARD

I am not heard within the womb
As mother lives through war
And, dodging bombs, flees London scenes
For Scotland's bonny shore.
So here I am a Highland lass
Born in my father's land
Whose fate is sealed by lack of sight.
Can no one understand?

My screams are heard by one and all
When, lifted to the breast,
I kick my legs and arch my back
In pain and gross protest.
Yet am I heard? No I am not!
A naughty baby, I
'Just leave her be, she'll go to sleep.'
And so I'm left to cry.

A twisted gut and further faults,
Revealed on an x-ray
Are impolite to talk about
So should be kept at bay.
And thus my childhood, rife with pain,
Is kept a secret, dark
Even from me, the naughty girl
On whom it makes its mark.

Children, though seen, should not be heard,
The motto of my time,
Is drummed into my aching mind:
To speak is but a crime.
And so to writing I must turn
To voice my hidden thought
The words I must not speak aloud
Are the pain with which I fought.

© Mel Menzies, 9th November, 2015

Author Notes

A recent Facebook discussion, within the Association of Christian Writers' group, cited how difficult it was to write memoir because of the inevitable mention of family members and friends. This was a dilemma I'd already had to face. Hence the blurb on the back of this book and the mention of the Drama Triangle at the end – which I've written more about on my website: http://www.melmenzies. co.uk/page/personal_growth_&_relationships_drama_triangle_&_ personality_type.

The problem is that it's all too easy to come across as a Victim; a 'poor me' inviting pity and compassion. Equally problematic, as I was only too well aware, is the concept of conveying an image of sainthood. A 'look at me and my faith – aren't you amazed?' when the reality is that I know myself to be a sinner not a saint.

So what to do? With my mother's death only weeks after I'd completed the writing of *Picked for a Purpose*, I wrestled with the dilemma for more than six months. Paramount in my mind was the idea of throwing the whole book out of the window. The professional reader's report had been more than favourable, but how could I risk the possibility of denouncement and alienation by my family? Worse still, what right do I have to reveal the behaviour – and its impact on me – of those I love?

Two things helped me decide. First was when I was asked by my rector if I would lead a house group for the elderly in a care home. Using the images and reflections of this book, I printed one-page studies for each chapter. Having witnessed, in my parents, the way in which long-term memory outweighs that of yesterday or last week, I've found that sharing my story verbally seems to arouse greater participation in the men and women in the group than an abstract Bible study. In addition, throughout that time I was reminded frequently by the Lord of the purpose for which he had created and saved me: namely to praise the one *who comforts us in all our troubles, so that we can comfort those in any trouble with the comfort we ourselves receive from God.*

And it was this conclusion that the ACW discussion brought forth. Without the revelation of aberrant behaviour throughout the Bible, we could not know the Word of God, nor the hope it offers to us all. Hence the story of my life which you have now read. The only proviso is that, as with all my previous books of testimony, I have changed names and places in order to protect those mentioned.

Also by Mel Menzies

Mel blogs regularly on her website **www.melmenzies.co.uk**.

Mel also writes, regularly, for Dr Steven Cangiano's website, Relationship Development & Transformation https://www.relationship-development.com/profile/melmenzies/

Time to Shine

The interweaving tale of counsellor Evie Adams and her client Julia Worth, a well-off 'lady of leisure', unhappily married to Carl. When Carl suspects Julia of being unfaithful, Julia's relationship becomes emotionally abusive and so her therapy sessions with Evie become an ever-increasing source of strength. Meanwhile, Hilary, a mutual friend of both Carl and Julia, seems to have been involved in a mysterious cover-up of a tragic death at Carl's school.

ISBN 9781910786055
Also available in eBook format

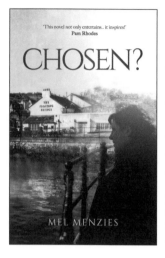

'This novel not only entertains.. it inspires!'
Pam Rhodes

CHOSEN?

MEL MENZIES

Chosen?

As a counsellor, based in Exeter's Cathedral Green, Evie Adams ponders the extraordinary circumstances surrounding her latest clients and the way they've impacted upon her own life. On the one hand is Phoebe, terrified that a distant relation is going to contest her deceased mother's will. On the other is Matt, seeking, with Evie's help, the mystery surrounding his biological parentage – all of which raises the question again and again as to whether adoption equates to being chosen or cheated.

ISBN: 9781910786321
Also available in ebook format